Your pee is important.

is

Jane

THE MISSING PIECE

DOING BUSINESS
THE DONATOS WAY

THE
MISSING
PIECE

DOING BUSINESS
THE DONATOS WAY

BY JANE GROTE ABELL

DONATOS®
Columbus, Ohio

First Edition

DONATOS

Columbus, Ohio
THE MISSING PIECE
by Jane Grote Abell

© 2015, Jane Grote Abell and Donatos,
All Rights Reserved.

No part of the contents of this book
may be reproduced by any means without
the written permission of the publisher.

Published by Donatos in conjunction with
The Ross Leadership Institute.
Columbus, Ohio 43230

www.donatos.com

Printed in the U.S.A.

ISBN: 978-0-9862159-1-9
Library of Congress Control Number: 2015948563

Book design by Carrie Cook

In Memory of :

My Grandparents

My grandparents served as role models for both sides of our family as entrepreneurs and servant leaders. They instilled a sense of pride and strong work ethic for generations to come.

Bill Rose

1945 - 2014

Bill served as our C.E.O. from 1999-2003. While you will read examples of my experiences under his leadership, he is a big reason that I had the courage to buy the company back with my dad. He believed in me and because of his passion to help others succeed he gave me courage. He pushed me in ways that tested my character and built me up in ways that gave me confidence. *His words to live by: Seek Help, Help Others, Be Teachable, Progress not Perfection, Patience, Surrender, Acceptance and Forgive Yourself.*

DEDICATION

I dedicate this book to my three children who
bring laughter, love and light into my life
every day. They inspire me daily with their
strength of character and Faith in the Lord.

To my husband and best friend Tom and my
three stepchildren. He brings me joy in life
and in business. He is my inspiration and my
biggest fan. He was my missing piece.

To my dad who taught me to love my
way through the tough days and
my mom who taught me about
second chances and compassion.

To my siblings who taught me that
transparency is the truest
measure of trust.

ACKNOWLEDGMENT

In memory of Paul Otte

1943 - 2015

Paul Otte served as the President of Franklin University, Columbus Ohio from 1986-2007. He became the Director of Franklin Leadership Center in 2012 and with the help of a local philanthropist Elizabeth "Libby" Ross, along with Debbie Johnson, Paul Founded The Ross Leadership Institute.

Paul was an esteemed author and dedicated his life to coaching, teaching, mentoring and helping others with a caring and humble attitude. His most recent book *WE Leadership,* published just a few months prior to his passing, is a perfect example of Paul's philosophy.

Paul is the reason I began my journey as an author. Not only did he encourage me to write a book based on my experiences, but he gave me the courage to write from my heart. He literally sat by my side week after week, with a pen in his hand and a smile on his face, eager to scratch notes on my manuscript. He was my mentor, my friend and my biggest fan. Paul had the ability to make everyone feel special in his presence because he was always present. His eyes would sparkle with excitement when he had a new idea. Paul had a contagious spirit. He had the ability to inspire self reflection and challenge without confrontation. His very presence brought a smile to my face and joy within my heart. Paul is the one person who persistently and relentlessly helped me write *The Missing Piece,* and now he is a piece that I am missing.

"While we are mourning the loss of our friend, others are rejoicing to meet him in Heaven"
–JOHN TAYLOR

x

TABLE OF CONTENTS

PIZZA SUBS SALADS

balance
DONATOS SUCCESS BEHAVIORS

 To be a principle-based, profitable Company dedicated to our Mission and Promise for 100 years and beyond.

 To promote goodwill through our Product and Service, Principles and People.

PRODUCT AND SERVICE

We believe that food served with love nourishes the soul. We believe Donatos is the best.

Only the highest quality and freshest ingredients are used to create consistently great tasting food in every restaurant, every day.

We believe in serving our Guests in the most friendly, caring way, in a clean and safe environment.

PRINCIPLES

We practice the Golden Rule of 'treating others the way that you would like to be treated.'

We believe in operating our business by the highest ethical standards.

Our Philosophy of Live, Love, Laugh and Learn is exercised to the mutual benefit of ALL.

Goodwill at Donatos is achieving a win-win outcome by just doing the right thing.

PEOPLE

We provide a fair, fun and caring atmosphere that promotes growth and development.

We encourage involvement in the communities in which we serve.

We attract Bold, Fun and Passionate Associates who truly care about serving Guests.

 To serve the best pizza and make your day a little better.

QUALITY AND TASTE

We promise to serve the highest quality, best-tasting pizza every time you order.

We apply generous toppings of the best ingredients from Edge to Edge® on our golden brown crust.

FRIENDLY AND HONEST SERVICE

We promise to serve your pizza with a smile and a "thank you" in clean, friendly restaurants.

Honest service means your order will be ready at the time promised for a fair price.

ASSOCIATES WHO CARE

We promise a fair, fun and caring atmosphere that promotes the growth and development of our Associates.

We strive to attract and coach good people who care about serving our Guests the best products.

GOOD NEIGHBOR

We promise to be a good neighbor by being a positive influence in the community.

That means conducting our business with respect for the community and maintaining our restaurants to be an asset to the neighborhood.

Symbolized by the passion we feel in our HEART. This is the entrepreneurial spirit that drives us to find opportunities, create excitement, build enthusiasm, act like an owner and accomplish tasks. Being entrepreneurial. Demonstrating optimism and creating positive energy. Being Guest focused. Listening to others' needs. Being honest and authentic. Smiling! Closing the sale. Willing to make mistakes by being aggressive and going for it. Taking action... and getting results. Motivating and inspiring others. Treating the restaurant as though you own it. Making work fun. Celebrating success. Being innovative. Exhibiting character. Being in the moment. Believing the best and taking risks.

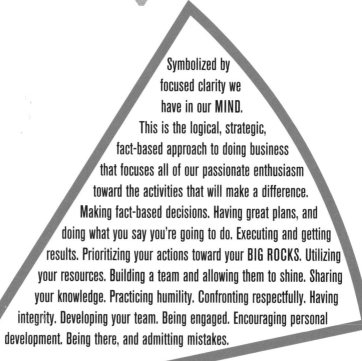

Symbolized by
focused clarity we
have in our MIND.
This is the logical, strategic,
fact-based approach to doing business
that focuses all of our passionate enthusiasm
toward the activities that will make a difference.
Making fact-based decisions. Having great plans, and
doing what you say you're going to do. Executing and getting
results. Prioritizing your actions toward your BIG ROCKS. Utilizing
your resources. Building a team and allowing them to shine. Sharing
your knowledge. Practicing humility. Confronting respectfully. Having
integrity. Developing your team. Being engaged. Encouraging personal
development. Being there, and admitting mistakes.

THE MISSING PIECE
By Jim Grote, Founder of Donatos

"Pizza made with love nourishes the soul."
–Jim Grote

This book is about free enterprise and what I believe is the missing piece– people with principles who have the courage to express them. I believe that business must be based not only on making a profit, but on integrating our innate human values and principles into its core. That core dictates why and how we operate. It is about Donatos Pizza, our family business as seen and experienced through the eyes of my daughter Jane.

I was 13 when I started working part time in the pizza business at a place called Cy's. During those six years I learned the basics of making pizza and operating a business. After starting out slicing pepperoni, making dough, and learning to bake the ovens, I managed two days a week when the owners took off work. The owners, Hollis and Cy, decided to split up and each open their own pizza place.

When they told me they were selling I was very sad. I really liked the guys and enjoyed my job. I learned everything about the pizza business from them, especially from Hollis. He was great and I can see him now, always smiling and kidding with us guys. He trusted us. We were all young kids working our first job and Hollis was a good role model. He was friendly and honest with the customers and suppliers, and fair with us... and he made a great pizza.

When he and Cy offered to sell me the business I was shocked. I never even thought about owning a business, especially at 16. I was going to school, playing football and basketball, and trying to get a date without having to dance. I was flattered that they actually thought I could own and operate the store.

The purchase price was $11,000, with no money down, and I could pay it off over five years. They decided to offer it to me before they put it on the market. With existing sales I could pay all the labor, food, rent and utilities, insurance and maintenance and still have plenty left over for the monthly payment. Now I was really excited! If only I could convince my dad....

Then reality set in. My dad insisted that I finish high school and go to college–of course he was right!–and they sold the business to another buyer. I was disappointed, but from then on I was determined that someday I would own my own business. Ironically I did end up acquiring Cy's, but not until my 20s.

I stayed on, working for the new owners, and I watched the workplace completely change from what I had experienced before. They didn't trust anyone and the workplace became toxic. The example set for the young kids was terrible and the business fell off. Every hour I worked I imagined how I would operate if I owned the business. I saw it work for Hollis–honesty, trust, fairness, treating customers, employees and vendors how they wanted to be treated, and making a great pizza.

While I was working part time at Cy's I attended The Ohio State University and took some business courses. There, I learned that the definition of business is "to produce goods and services for the sole purpose of making a profit." I already knew that there was a lot more to business than just making money.

In the summer of 1963 as a sophmore, I dropped
out of college to finally buy my own business,
Donatos. I was going to run the business with the
values and principles I had learned at home, at
school and at my first job or else I would quit
and go back to college and become an accountant.
When I started out, all of my mentors–the
construction workers, body shop guys and
plumbers who were advising me–would say
that business is "dog eat dog" and if I brought
the principles that I believed in into business, I
wouldn't make it.

Did that mean I had to leave my principles at
home so I could make money? Was business just
for making money or could it be more? What I
learned during the years I worked at Cy's formed
the foundation for how I would operate Donatos. I
was going to prove that being competitive doesn't
mean that you can't be fair and honest, that
treating your employees and suppliers with trust
and respect doesn't mean you're soft, that treating
customers the way I would like to be treated was
the best approach to business, and I could do this
and make a profit doing it.

On the first day we had customers waiting in
line to buy pizza, motivated by a 25 cents off
coupon. The line extended down the block as they
waited for us to open at 5:00 p.m. I was excited
yet terrified as we opened the door and began
taking our first orders for pizza. That first night
was so busy that my memory of it is a blur, but the
customers kept coming back. My dream of owning
my own business had become a reality and I was
not quite 20 years old.

Every day was busier than the last and my
commitment to the golden rule became harder
and harder to live up to. I worked one hundred
hours a week and still fell short of my goal. I
would remember, after we closed for the night,
the customers we let down and wondered if they
would come back again. If I took a night off I would
get a headache wondering if the customers were
being treated the way I wanted to be treated.
I was becoming a slave to my commitment but
I never thought of giving up. If we fell short of
our goal we would get up the next day, brush
ourselves off and start again. But we would never,
never lower the bar.

DONICE FORAKER
Manager Menu/Equipment Development–*Trouble shooter*

"My family lived in the neighborhood just blocks away from the first store. My older brother worked there first. I started in 1966 when I was 13 and have been here ever since. It was always about a quality product at a fair price with good service.

Because it was a cash business you need to trust in people. That's why Jim felt you had to hire good people to open stores. I think that's what led to the belief that everybody's part of the business and you have to respect their opinions. I became manager of the Worthington store in '78 and more of a 'trouble shooter' ever since."

WILLY WEBB
Director of Quality, Jane's Dough Foods—*It was a clubhouse*

"I got my first job at Donatos in 1968. I was 14 years old and Jim hired me to clean pizza pans for $10 a week. I worked there all through high school doing all kinds of jobs. After high school, I became a delivery driver, then around 1974, I decided to make a career out of it and became a store manager. I spent my first 20 years in the original store.

When all of us who were here at the beginning— Grote, Donice Foraker, Roger Howard and others— talk about the early days I say it wasn't really a job, it was a clubhouse. All of our school friends worked there at one time or another. It was a lot of fun.

Jim Grote encouraged us to grow personally and professionally, and gave us the opportunity to make a better life for our families and ourselves. Plus, I've been able to eat pizza every day for the last 45 years. I'm a pizza lover through and through, so it has been a real pleasure, believe me."

ROGER HOWARD
Franchise Partner, RTJ Restaurants–
It's the greatest job in the world

"I wouldn't trade working at Donatos for anything in the world. I started in 1967 when I was 14 years old. There was a group of us. We would hang out at the store during the day, 'off the clock' making supplies for the night. Half of us had keys. We always had fun.

Jim's integrity was noticeable. It made you want to work for him. I remember at the first store on Thurman Avenue, the cash register didn't always work, so we put the money in a drawer until the end of the night. Jim trusted us. At 22, I was the General Manager at Tamarack Circle (Store #3). I was responsible for everything–payroll, purchasing and paying the bills.

Things started to grow in the mid-80s when we started advertising on TV. In the mid-90s we all got together to plan. That's when we started franchising. By 1998 I was VP for Operations and Tom Grote was the COO. It was my passion–we did everything with the Promise in mind. Donatos lets people make mistakes. Whatever you do, if you do it with integrity and honesty, you can't be wrong."

It was the 70s. By then I was married, raising a family, and living behind the store. The business was profitable and sales were growing every week even though the pizza was good but inconsistent, deliveries were slow, and wait times were way too long. It wasn't the way I wanted to be treated as a customer. I needed to come up with a system that would make a consistent pizza every time, on time.

I took only the salary I needed and invested the rest in developing a system that allowed us to grow and take better care of our customers. We added phone lines so customers wouldn't be put on hold. To ensure consistency, we purchased digital scales that allowed us to weigh every topping as we made each pizza. We printed our order tickets listing the weight next to each topping for every item on the menu. We were among the first pizza companies to install conveyor ovens, and we developed special pans that would bake as well and twice as fast as the old deck ovens.

By the early 1980s we had developed a system designed for high volume to allow for on time pizza consistently no matter how busy we were. We were able to train anyone to consistently produce the same great tasting pizza that we made in 1963. This allowed us to grow and build many Donatos in the Columbus area, and eventually franchise throughout the region.

My four kids had grown up in the business, working part time as soon as they were old enough. My oldest son Tom majored in business and finance at Miami University of Ohio and decided to join Donatos full time working in our stores. Tom implemented the principles we use every day in operating Donatos. When Tom became COO, he wanted to capture what we were trying to achieve in a mission statement so that everyone knew what our company was about.

We operated with principles and the golden rule but what did that mean? With input from me, Jane, the family and key employees, we crafted a mission statement that included all of the things we were the most passionate about–operating our business with principles, providing a great product, hiring the right people, providing the best service and promoting goodwill by being a good neighbor in the community.

Our Mission

"To promote goodwill through our product and principles, people and service."

In 1993 my son Tom helped structure our franchise program. When we started franchising I was very parental, not wanting to give up control over who was making our pizza. Tom brought our franchise partners into our strategy for growth–keeping our principles and making a profit. He stressed that the value of franchising relies on being a partner in our business. They were investing their money into our system and principles. Their success would propel our success. Tom's approach was right for the franchise community and Donatos.

Jane also came on board right after college, first working in the training department with her mother Nancy. Jane and Nancy brought a sorely needed feminine energy and compassion to Donatos. They brought a woman's perspective to our training and management style. Jane simply excelled in that area. Together Jane and her mom brought concern for people front and center.

Where I was intense about building our system, Jane and her mom brought empathy, compassion and caring to the table. In the beginning I was strict, more "old school", about what we should expect from ourselves and associates–show up on time, do your job, no whining–leave your moods at home. Jane's approach was different. She tried to understand the people she was dealing with and work with them. Her interest in our people was as intense as my interest in our product and she was relentless in her advocacy of the "people first" approach.

Jane was able to see that the system doesn't make the pizza. The people make the pizza. And if the people don't care about what they are doing, even with a great system the pizza won't taste the same every time. Jane brought the head and the heart of our business together.

Over time we attracted attention from the world's largest restaurant company, McDonald's. After searching around the world, they chose Donatos as the "best in class" pizza to be part of their meal occasion strategy. We sold to McDonald's in 1999. I was very excited and I knew that because they had the infrastructure, they could grow our principle-based company around the world. I even believed our business philosophy would influence their culture. How egotistical is that!

Four years later we found ourselves with the opportunity to buy the company back. We knew that out people were still in place in the stores and we could still fulfill our mission. We bought Donatos back in 2003 and Jane became president.

Looking back, I see how special our people and culture are and how close we came to losing it. McDonald's bought the concept but couldn't capture the soul of Donatos. I didn't realize that our soul and spirit was waning during those years and that our credibility with our associates, franchise community and customers was damaged. After we bought it back, Jane visited every store and personally promised them that we would ensure the values that our company was founded on.

I never realized how hard it would be to build a profitable business based on the Golden Rule, but after 50 years I know it can be done. Donatos will continue to be a principle based company, making a profit and striving to fulfill our mission: "To promote goodwill though our products, principles, people and service" and through our profit strive to create prosperity. For me, prosperity is longer term and inclusive. It means the well-being of everyone–our people, our customers and our community.

Jane has the mission of the company built into her core. From her start in the training department, she advanced to the Chief People Officer, to President and COO, and now Chairwoman of Donatos. She is in great demand as a speaker, has received numerous awards, sits on many non-profit boards in Columbus and has dedicated her life to helping Donatos strive to realize the ideals and values the company was founded on.

Jane's leadership has not only preserved our culture but has taken it to another level, by inspiring our people to express our principles through character, courage, conviction and compassion. I am proud of her accomplishments and excited that she has now put her ideas and beliefs into book form to share what she has learned, and to share the values and ideals that have inspired her throughout her life. ♥

LIANNE McCLADE
Director Guest Services, Donatos
Pizza–*Jim's vision was compelling*

"Most of us are here because Jim's vision was so compelling. He would just sweep you along with the strength of his vision. From the first time you're exposed to it, you're like, 'I'm all in, just tell me what you need and tell me where we're going.' He could make you want it as badly as he did–you just wanted to help make it happen.

Jim genuinely wants everyone to be as successful in their work as he is. He wants us to love it as much as he does. He wants our kids to come work for Donatos. He wants us to be family forever, which could be why so many people have been with the organization for so long. Vision is a powerful thing."

CHAPTER 1
A REALLY GOOD PRODUCT

I don't think of myself as a leader or an author. So it was very difficult for me to think about writing any book, especially one on leadership. But after a presentation I made on **Bringing Your Principles to Work,** one of the participants asked, "Will you be writing a book based on your leadership philosophy?"

I was surprised, but I was told that within an hour after the presentation there were already several messages offering to buy the book. And since then many people have continued to encourage me to write it. Although it took longer than I expected, what follows is the result. As you will see, it is more about "our" story than my leadership.

I see myself on a journey of becoming a leader. Along the way I've found that it's about your beliefs, your behaviors and results. All these things have come together through my experiences–learning about character, courage, conviction and compassion. I've learned a lot about what to do and what not to do from life experiences. However, my best mentors have always been my father and mother.

Most of what I've learned, good and bad, comes from my family. My father started working when he was 13, living in the south end of Columbus, Ohio, at the corner of Deshler and Parsons. He has only had three jobs his entire life: paperboy, plumber and pizza maker. So I'm following in his footsteps with pizza; I have not yet mastered the skill of a plumber or a papergirl.

When Dad started working in a pizza place at 13, he had some life altering experiences that guided him and set the foundation for how he wanted to run his own business one day. As a teenage boy he grew up Catholic, in a very principle centered home. His dad served in the Army and upon his return, he owned and operated his own grocery store. My dad would take the bus, at age eight, to help his dad stock the shelves and bag the groceries.

My dad had a love for comic books and super heroes. He would ride the bus, and sometimes get so caught up in the comic book that he would miss his bus stop. My grandfather ended up closing his grocery business but it is obvious that entrepreneurship runs deep in our family history. My mom's dad owned and operated his own plumbing business, Baumann Plumbing.

My grandma Grote stayed at home with their five children. After my grandfather closed the grocery store he worked as a butcher and worked hard to make ends meet. My dad will tell stories of watching his mom count pennies to pay the bills. My dad knew at an early age the value of a work ethic, having principles, and showing up to work on time.

> *"Whether a job is big or small, do it right, or not at all.*
> *"Once a job has first begun, do it right until it's done."*
> **'Grandpa' Grote**

Dad went from carrying papers at age 13 to working at Cy's Pizza. This is where he learned the lesson of bringing your principles to work. During his experiences he worked for two distinctly different owners.

One owner was a man of great integrity. Everything this manager did was with honesty and authenticity and treating the employees and customers right. He always made sure the pizzas were the same every time they were made. On the nights when he worked the customers and employees were happy and business was good.

The other owner dad worked for was not necessarily a person with the "most integrity." His character may have been a little flawed. So when the cash would come in, sometimes instead of going in the register it would go in his pocket. He would go to the bar and pick up women and bring them back to the pizza kitchen. He cut corners on the quality of the pizzas, watering down the sauce or scrimping on the pepperoni. He would tell raunchy jokes to the workers and didn't trust them. Dad quickly learned that on the nights this owner worked fewer people ordered pizzas.

Starting at the age of 13, my dad was watching and learning about life and integrity from both of these owners. At that very young age, he could recognize the differences between the two owners and their approaches to the business.

He learned that doing the right thing for the customer and employees paid off. He saw for himself that on the nights the owner treated the customers and employees right, the business was growing. As a result of Dad's experiences, we take huge pride in and today still hire 14 and 15 year olds for the very same reason–to make sure we teach the next generation about honesty, integrity and strength of character.

At 16, Dad had an opportunity to buy the business. One of the owners wanted out and told my dad, "I'm going to let the business run down so I can buy his partner out at a lower price." This seemed contradictory to what my dad had observed in business. Dad wanted to own his own business so he could bring his principles to work with him. So he went home to his dad and said, "I know I am 16, playing football and have a couple more years of school, but if you'll just help me out on Friday nights after football I can buy this place and own my own business."

My grandpa looked at him and said, "Jim, pizza is just a fad, it's not going to go anywhere. You need to stay in school, go to college and get your degree." Although disappointed, my dad remained passionate about building a business on principles. So he continued to work through high school and into college.

My dad on the football field at age 16.

When he was about 20, a student at The Ohio State University and still working at Cy's pizza shop, he found himself in a position where the owner of Donatos wanted to sell and said he'd sell it to the first person to come up with the money. This time the owner of the business was a man of great integrity. His name was Don Potts and his approach to business was in alignment with my father's principles. By this time, Dad had more experience and was passionate about owning his own business.

He was learning in school that the 'sole purpose of owning a business was to produce goods and services for the sole purpose of making a profit". This business philosophy was not capturing the spirit in which my dad wanted to own his business. So he approached his father and future father-in-law about the opportunity. My grandpa and dad's future father-in-law (my mom's dad) loaned him the money, and with $1,300 my dad was in business and Donatos was born.

JIM BAUMANN
Jim Grote's Former Brother-In-Law–
It was good to have friends

"When Jim Grote was a young guy, he worked for my dad's plumbing company during the day and for a pizza place at night. He was dating my sister at the time and was close to our family. My dad took Jim over to make his pitch to buy the pizza business from Don Potts, which served Kelly's bar next door and people in the neighborhood.

The business amounted to not much more than an oven and a couple of pieces of equipment. Don had already been approached to sell the business to other people, but my dad and Jim convinced him to sell it to them.

Jim got his brothers to move the equipment to the space in front of my dad's plumbing shop. My dad was glad to have a tenant and wanted to help Jim get a good start. We plumbed it for him overnight and installed the oven the next morning. We got the place wired and the equipment hooked up–all Jim paid for was the vent pipe, and even that got installed for free. It was good to have friends who could help him get set up.

And the next day he was selling pizza! There was a line out the door. Everyone was holding these sheets of paper my sister had given them to get them to come buy a pizza for a dollar. One day a while after he moved the business across the street to the location in front of his house, I remember he ran upstairs to the plumbing shop and told me, 'I just did a $5,000 Friday!' Not a $5,000 week but in one day.

Jim was so excited. That was when you could see that things were really happening. Eventually that store was doing $2 million a year."

Keeping in mind that my dad was not Italian and recognizing that Grote Pizza would not be the best name for a pizza place, dad bought the name Donatos from Don Potts. He was a good man and former seminarian. Don Potts named his establishment Donatos because the Latin derivative means "to give a good thing". At an early age my dad recognized the importance of a name and didn't get caught up in his ego of naming the business after himself. The message, to give a good thing, was more important.

Dad with Don Potts. Dad bought the name Donatos from Don Potts, which means "to give a good thing".

The signed agreement between Dad and Don Potts to buy Donatos.

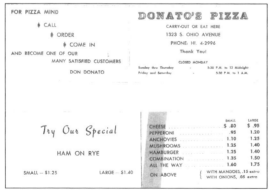

A copy of the front & back of a 1958 menu of Donatos Pizza when Don Potts owned it.

FOR PIZZA MIND

♦ CALL

♦ ORDER

♦ COME IN

AND BECOME ONE OF OUR

MANY SATISFIED CUSTOMERS

DON DONATO

DONATO'S PIZZA

CARRY-OUT OR EAT HERE

1323 S. OHIO AVENUE

PHONE: HI. 4-2996

Thank You!

CLOSED MONDAY

Sunday thru Thursday - 5:30 P.M. to 12 Midnight

Friday and Saturday - 5:30 P.M. to 1 A.M.

𝒯ry 𝒪ur 𝒮pecial

HAM ON RYE

SMALL — $1.25   LARGE — $1.40

	SMALL	LARGE
CHEESE	$ .80	$ .95
PEPPERONI	.95	1.20
ANCHOVIES	1.10	1.25
MUSHROOMS	1.25	1.40
HAMBURGER	1.25	1.40
COMBINATION	1.35	1.50
ALL THE WAY	1.60	1.75
ON ABOVE	{ WITH MANGOES, .15 extra	WITH ONIONS, .05 extra

30

THE EARLY YEARS

My dad wanted to open his first restaurant based on The Golden Rule. He was determined to prove that you could build a business based on principles. While he had some early experiences in business that taught him what not to do, they were certainly defining moments. He knew that by putting all the cash in the drawer, paying taxes, reinvesting the rest in people and the business, the business would prosper.

Our Mission: Dad's mission in business was to build a business based on the Golden Rule, to treat others the way you would want to be treated. Today, our mission is to promote good will through our product, our principles, our service and our people. We try to bring our mission alive at the store level so our associates can understand how to live it through their actions.

Our Promise: to serve the best pizza and make our customer's day a little better. It's really the operating manual for our store managers and associates. That was Dad's goal when he began. It was our passion when our family got involved in the business.

My dad opened his first pizza shop in a store room in front of my grandpa's plumbing shop on Thurman Avenue, Columbus, Ohio. My grandma made the dough in her kitchen; his brothers and my uncles helped work in the business. My grandparents also made the sausage and meatballs. Even today the smell of the sausage reminds me of my grandma. The business was a labor of love for the family from the very start.

And even while the business was booming, my father had the vision to expand the business. After work he would sit on the front windowsill and he would visualize a building across the street, filled with happy people. He would visualize a black brick building in the middle of this residential area. Here sits this pizza place that he visualized every day–customers coming in with smiles on their faces, the associates happy, the entire environment, creating and feeling the energy.

Sometimes people say, "What a dreamer", but the reality is he's a man of great vision. He also put the hard work in to make it happen. So out of his vision, out of the things he aspired to make happen, his conviction and passion to build this black brick building, he did it! And over 50 years later it is still one our top 10 restaurants in the entire company.

Dad was so adamant in getting black bricks because he said that is what he saw in his vision every night. So he traveled to London, Ohio, for the black brick. He built the pizza store and shortly after bought the house located immediately behind the restaurant that became our home.

The black brick building—Dad's first store on Thurman Avenue in Columbus, Ohio.

So many of our childhood memories come from living behind the restaurant. I cherish those memories but now that I have kids I realize it wasn't necessarily a normal childhood experience. Our front yard was the back of the restaurant, so we grew up running the spaghetti sauce my mom made over to the store.

My dad would run to my grandma's house to pick up the meatballs and sausage. My brother started sweeping the parking lot at age five. It was a constant part of our lives.

The employees were like family. A number of them are still working with Donatos to this day. Dad hired a special group of high school kids, Willy Webb, Donice Foraker and Roger Howard. These three individuals have dedicated their entire lives to the Mission of our family business. They all have stories about their first work experience that became a way of life for each one of them. They never wavered on their loyalty to doing the right thing and my dad treated them as though they were younger brothers. They would continuously pick on the four of us kids by locking us in the walk-in cooler, putting fish in our plastic swimming pool, and giving us lettuce when my mom asked us to go to the store to get Mangoes (green peppers). It was an environment that I loved. It was a wonderful experience. Part of the rich experience included entertaining our customers.

Dad with Donatos' first crew.

When my dad visualized that black brick building, for whatever reason, he did not visualize a dining room. When people would come to pick up their pizza, every night he would say, "Your pizza isn't ready, go back and see Nancy and the kids." They would write "B.A.G." on the order for Back At Grotes. Mom always opened the door with a smile and welcomed the families into our home. So every night our living room was full of customers. It was a wonderful experience. Imagine, learning what hospitality is really all about by asking people to come into your home.

Donatos customers waiting for their pizzas in our family's living room.

They would sit and eat with us. We'd get to know their kids. We have so many memories and many of those customers are still customers today. There were times I'd wake up in the morning, getting ready for school, and they were all still in our home. There was a constant flow of people coming into our home and becoming part of our lives.

My sister and I shared a room and we had a little picture window that overlooked the restaurant. When my dad bought the business he bought his first sign. It was one of those really big signs with an arrow on it that blinked. Although it was eye catching, it certainly lit up the neighborhood. I remember staying up past our bedtime, watching all the commotion right outside our picture window. Little did I know this window would be my window to the world, my future and what is now my passion in life.

My brother Tom and me on the front porch of our family home behind the first Donatos location.

With my siblings in front of the first Donatos on Thurman Avenue.

My sister Katie and me playing in the yard we shared with the first Donatos.

Sometimes at night my dad would come to get us and we'd stand under that sign and I remember he would say, "One day we're going to have our pizza places all around the world." But he never stopped there, he didn't talk about how much money he wanted to make or mention that he wanted to be the biggest. He always said, "We're going to be around the world, and be a business with principles; we're going to teach people in our business and create an environment for our kids to learn about honesty, integrity and the importance of coming to work on time."

The first Donatos Pizza sign.

And that has been his passion ever since. There
were four of us growing up together. I have an older
brother, a younger sister and younger brother, and
over the years we have all worked in the family
business. My mom started out making the spaghetti
sauce for the business. But her real talent was the
people side of the business. She taught us that
our customers and associates were our family. She
knew early on that opening her home flamed the
spirit of the business. As we grew the business,
she went back to college and started our Human
Resources (HR) department. She also led our Real
Estate Department. She picked the majority of
our restaurant locations. She has a keen sense
of knowing whether or not a restaurant location
would be successful. I still consult with my mom
on all my real estate decisions to this day. My mom
brought the human factor to the business. She has
a unique ability to empathize with people but hold
them accountable.

We all grew up working in the restaurants
through high school and college. My older brother
Tom was the one that came back from college and
developed our strategy for growth. Tom is the
one that influenced us to write down our mission

statement for the first time along with our promise. He truly understood the processes for not just the making of the pizza, but how to lead an operations department. Ultimately Tom became our COO.

Tom really deserves a lot of the credit for the growth and the expansion of the family business. Under his leadership we spent an entire year ensuring the proper training of our people in the stores before we went on television. He's the one that led the efforts in franchising. He was constantly pushing the growth envelope, always searching for ways we were going to grow. I would define myself as his right hand person. We were good partners and we worked really well together but he always took the lead. He was the visionary. Because of his vision, he probably helped me have a greater vision and taught me to stretch myself beyond what I thought was possible.

My dad always had the vision for growth and my brother put the efforts behind how we were really going to do it. Tom always would say to me, "You know you can learn this, you have passion for it, you know you can do this." When I graduated from

The Ohio State University, I started working in our training department. A few years later, I decided to interview for the human resource position. I remember I was a single mom raising my son Tony when I interviewed with my mom and dad for the position. I was nervous but I was passionate about our people. I knew at an early age that the people in the company make up the heart of the company. My mom taught me how to balance having a heart and head in the family business.

Katie, my younger sister, and I grew up side by side. Like we all did, she grew up in the business. She started in our commissary, cracking eggs, making pizzas, working with our grandma. She also worked in the restaurants so she could understand what it's like to run and manage a store. She has that gentle strength about her. If you ask anyone around her they will say that she's the nicest person without a doubt.

Katie has real empathy about her. She can really feel other people's energy. When she got out of college she worked in catering. She brought a creative energy to catering and led our catering efforts into the new markets. And like the rest of us, my much younger brother Kyle grew up in the business, working in the restaurants at an early age folding boxes and later in our Marketing Department. He is a creative and passionate person who challenges all of us to think differently about life and love. He brings joy to those around him and believes in living with peace, love and happiness.

CONSISTENCY ISN'T BORING

In a perfect world, everyone should get to love what they do, feeling deeply rewarded by the work itself and the meaningful engagement with others. In an even more perfect world, they'd also love their product so much that work would be just another way to tell people how much enthusiasm they feel for the product in the first place. That's what we like to see at Donatos.

Since the very earliest days of our company—when it was my dad running just the one restaurant in front of our house—the quality of our product has been a top priority. From his own experience working in a pizza place as a teenager, he knew how a pizza made with the highest quality ingredients and prepared with love would define the value of a customer's experience.

In the beginning, with just one store and my dad's hands on just about every order, he could personally ensure the quality of his product. From the start my dad insisted on the highest quality possible ingredients and a process that ensured that the customer would always be served a pizza that was just as good as the last pizza he bought from us. It's all part of our promise–to serve the best pizza and make our customer's day better with the highest quality ingredients and consistent pizza every time. Yet my dad learned the hard way how complicated it can be to actually deliver on that promise.

He opened two additional stores in the late 60s, but he quickly learned that he didn't have the process in place to deliver on a consistent pizza. Late at night he would get phone calls from customers telling him how the other store ran out of pepperoni and instead substituted salami on the pizza, or ran out of provolone and used Romano cheese as a substitute. Because he didn't feel he had the systems in place to fulfill the promise to deliver a consistent pizza to his customers, he closed those stores.

He continued to run the original Donatos; at the same time he was painstakingly developing the standards that would guarantee the promise of the ongoing customer experience he envisioned. Not once did my dad waiver in his vision of building a business based on principles. He didn't see closing these two stores as a failure; he viewed it as an opportunity to improve his system for making pizza. He said he would never open another pizza place until he could do it with consistency, making sure the right process was in place. It was his unwritten contract with the customers–once they bought a pizza they would get the same quality pizza every time.

He focused on establishing and refining systems that would allow him to train people to do things consistently, from making the pizzas, to baking and serving them, to running a store. He refused to even consider opening another store until he had systems he believed in and a well-trained manager to run the place. It wasn't just a matter of hiring more people, but rather looking for processes and even the equipment that would let him ensure consistency.

Inspired by books, he read *The Power of Positive Thinking, Think and Grow Rich* and, later in life, *The Goal.* My dad always treated the restaurant like a little manufacturing plant! He was able to identify the process bottlenecks that challenged consistency and he would either invest in the right equipment to solve the issue or innovate a new piece of equipment to solve the problem. He wouldn't stop until he found a solution.

PASSION + PERSEVERANCE + POSITIVE THINKING = PROSPERITY

For example, the Pepp-A-Matic was born during this period of systems development. When he started his own business, he was using hand-crank deli slicers to slice the pepperoni, but he insisted on using the same amount of pepperoni on each pizza and that became one of his biggest obstacles. By slicing the pepperoni by hand, there would be some slices that were thicker than other slices. Since we weigh all of our toppings, the pizza would look inconsistent. The Pepp-A-Matic was my dad's ingenious solution to another problem that he was determined to solve.

The original Pepp-A-Matic.

My dad created a prototype slicer behind our house and brought it into the restaurant. It was a manual machine at the time. His passion for consistency didn't stop at slicing the pepperoni; he was determined to ensure that every piece had the same amount of toppings for every pizza. This literally kept my dad up at night. He developed a system where scales are used to weigh the pizzas as they are being assembled. Each ingredient is added with an exact weight requirement. This allowed every pizza to have the very same amount of each ingredient, ensuring a consistent end result. He would work tirelessly with the associates to figure out the exact weight on every piece, to ensure there would be the same amount of toppings and every bite would taste the same.

Dad was so committed to the quality of the product that he bought a scale in the early 1970s that cost $2,000–the price of an oven. Toppings and dough are weighed to a 100th of a pound. It allowed for our "edge to edge" signature. It also allows associates– no matter where they work or how much experience they have–to assemble every pizza in exactly the same way. Some 50 years later, our associates still build our pizza to exact specifications, right on a scale.

That's where the Pepp-A-Matic is equally important– by assuring consistency in the pepperoni slices. Ironically we never ended up using the Pepp-A-Matic in restaurants. It turns out the equipment was better suited for the frozen pizza industry. The Grote Manufacturing Company was founded in 1972 and brings leading food processing solutions, like the Pepp-A-Matic, to companies worldwide.

In another example, Dad knew the ovens were a bottleneck. The old deck turn-style ovens slowed the time it took to bake a pizza. In addition, they allowed for inconsistency. They needed to be working with faster ovens that were timed for a consistent bake every time.

It didn't matter how many extra people you hired to work a busy Friday or Saturday night–you couldn't do more business if your slow ovens were holding you back. So after a lot of investigation and research, Dad replaced his double-deck ovens with conveyor ovens that baked more pizzas at once, and also provided the consistency he was looking for on the baked crust. Each belt has a unique time and temperature to perfectly cook all pizza regardless of the thickness of the crust or number of toppings.

While others may have what is considered an occupation, my dad has always had a "preoccupation" with the quality of our ingredients. And he instilled it in every team member and family member.

Another example of investing in technology to solve inconsistency problems was how we made our dough. We used to make our dough in every restaurant.

Unfortunately, depending on who was making the dough for the day, the ingredients would vary from store to store and the pizzas would taste different. Donice Foraker, who has been with us from the beginning, has been responsible for the quality of our dough for over 49 years. We refer to him as "Dr. Dough."

DONICE FORAKER
**Manager Menu/Equipment
Development, Donatos Pizza–**
The same ready-to-go dough

"In 1990, we were having problems rolling the dough consistently and the equipment we were using kept breaking down. I thought we needed to come up with a process that would allow us to sheet the dough ourselves and ship it to the stores so that every store was using the same ready-to-go dough. I went to a bakery show, met some people, looked at some equipment, and started testing some possibilities in the commissary.

Grote saw what I was doing and said we had to hurry this up. I told him I needed to be able to test the dough in one store, a store I knew well. So we shipped the dough to this one store every day, giving it about a year to work out the kinks. Sales were up 20 percent in that store, which was great, but it was also interesting to discover that the store was easier to keep clean without all the flour flying around all day.

When we were ready to expand the process to other stores, we didn't have the capacity to do it for all of them. So we added just five stores at first, seeing the same jump in sales and an improvement in service too. The trick was in figuring out just the right timing on each leg of the process. We had to buy new equipment to pull this off, but it really changed everything for us and for the stores."

In addition to ensuring that the quality of the dough consistently tasted great, my dad went to great measures to ensure that the specifications for the toppings met his high quality standards. He was passionate to find suppliers (we call them Business Partners) who would work with his precise specifications for the cheese, pepperoni and sausage. Meeting those specifications was key to getting the consistency he expected. He was willing to pay more for the best ingredients because he believed that the costs of the better ingredients would be recouped in the long-term dollar value of customer loyalty.

Dad's devotion to a perfectly consistent product has carried through to every item that's on our menu– from the seven kinds of pizza he served on his first day in business, through the development of our specialty pizzas, subs and salads over the years. In the early days, he would sit with Donice Foraker, Roger Howard and Willy Webb to make up different types of pizzas or other products and then try them out in the kitchen.

One of the things I love about our Donatos family is how proud they have been of our product from the beginning. I think that is a direct result of the time and care my dad put into establishing such a high standard for what we do from the beginning. People want to believe in the value of their work; they want to be able to point to the results of their efforts and say, "We did that." And even though my dad established these standards for his own reasons, he also created a culture of excellence around our business that our associates, managers and executive team take personally too.

The fact is, once you make a pizza to my dad's consistent quality standards, you never want to do it another way. His standard becomes yours because the proof of its value is right there with our happy customers. The satisfaction of providing a consistent product along with respectful customer service is pretty compelling once you get a taste for it.

TODD YOUNG
**VP Company Operations,
Donatos Pizza–*Why we hire*
*14 and 15 year olds***

*"I started with Donatos when I was 15 years old
in 1979. Donice Foraker who was General Manager
of the Worthington (our 4th) store hired me. My
reasons for joining Donatos were simple–I lived in
Worthington so it was convenient and I liked the
pizza. I kept working at the Worthington store after
high school and into college. What kept me here for
35 years is a longer story.*

*At one point I had to ask myself–do I continue on
with my schooling, that I didn't like, or focus on a
career at Donatos? I asked Jim for his advice and he
told me whatever I decided he would support me.
He didn't try and steer me one way, or another.
He just encouraged me to pursue my passion, my
dream. And that's what I have done ever since and
it's what I tell others. I think it helps to elevate the
level of engagement of the people that work here.*

*People ask why we hire 14 and 15 year olds? I believe
those who think working with them is a hassle have*

never worked with them the way we do. It's both a blessing and a responsibility. They are limited in what they can do, but they are enthusiastic because they are working. They have a smile and our customers like them. I encourage each General Manager to have 1 to 3 as part of their 20 to 30 associates (10-15 percent).

By the time they are 16 they are generally making more than the minimum wage, are ingrained in our culture, and loyal. Most will stay with us through high school and college, returning to work when they can. Both my daughters started at 14 and worked with us over 10 years. Many come back to us after college because they like and believe in what we do. Others will move on, but many carry our values with them. They are transferable to most businesses.

Jim put a stake in the ground in 1963 regarding our values and putting the customer and our people first. I could tell you hundreds of examples where we made decisions based on that and our promise. Other companies might focus on short-term profits, but we have always believed that our values and following our promise would result in steady growth over time. It makes me proud."

Mom with Todd Young circa 1988.

THE GROWTH YEARS

We started Donatos in 1963 and throughout the 70s we focused on innovation to maintain consistency. We hired some critical people during this time that would grow with our company. Eleanor White, affectionately known as 'Whitie', was brought on board as our bookkeeper. She had just retired from another company and Dad talked her into working part-time. Whitie worked full time and ended up retiring 25 years later! During these years we were fortunate to attract people who would end up dedicating their entire lives to Donatos and many of them are all still with us today. My uncle Jim Baumann worked with my dad in the early days and later joined us after he retired from Public Office to oversee our maintenance. My cousin Matt Baumann and John Grote who started with us as hourly associates ran restaurants and opened new markets. Charlene Rose was recruited to start up our Catering Department and became my first boss after I graduated from college. Phyllis Rucker and Ruth Bell worked in our Commissary with my grandma and grandpa. They were all with us over 30 years and contributed so much to who we are as a company. While we were a family business the family was much wider than being directly related. There are a number of people who started with us in their teenage years, like Tim Young our current Director of Franchise Business Development and Todd Young who is currently VP of Company Operations.

Eleanor White, affectionately known as 'Whitie,' on her last day with Donatos.

DONATOS HISTORY

1963

Jim Grote buys
Thurman Ave.
aka South at
20 years of age

1974

Commissary
& Bakery

1987

15 Stores
Television

1989

Party Plannir
Catering

2001

Philadelphia
Orlando

2002

Smithsonian
Germany
207 Stores

2003

Founding
Family
Buys Back
Donatos

2004

Take & Bal
No Dough
Pizza

1993

Cincinnati
Dayton
Kentucky

1995-1998

Indianapolis
Canton
Michigan
Cleveland
Atlanta
140 Stores

1999

Acquisition by
McDonald's
143 Stores

2005

Ready to Use
Dough
Cutting Edge
Concept

2008

45th
Anniversary

2009

Kroger Atlanta T&B Opens
Fry's Food Rolls Take & Bake
326 Take & Bake Outlets
Hand-Tossed Pizza

Roger Howard and John Grote.

Charlene Rose, the former head of our Catering Department, current franchise partner of three restaurants and my first boss after I graduated from college.

In memory of Ruth Bell, shown here with my mother, who worked in our Commissary with my grandma and grandpa.

The 1980s were about identifying and implementing our processes and our systems. We had grown to 22 restaurants and that meant a lot of changes to what we were doing. For example, we installed gas ovens at each location. That was a major expenditure, a real commitment for us. To be consistent in our approaches across all stores, we created training manuals and policies for managing the business. I worked in the training department with Charlene Rose, Tim Young and Curtis Elder* where we certified training stores and worked side by side with our new managers.

The greatest change during the 80s may have been in the introduction of technology and the investment in our Point of Sale Systems. My brother led the efforts to introduce a new POS system in our restaurants. We could not find a system that would calculate our specifications for weights so we developed our own proprietary POS, which we still use today.

Another significant event of the 80s was our decision to go on television. Our sales grew by 26 percent that year because of our TV advertising. We learned a lot about marketing. The growth continued into the 90s as we started expanding. We began the decade with 35 stores in 1990. In '93 we entered the Cincinnati market. My cousin Matt Baumann who worked for the family business for 35 years opened our first market outside of Columbus, Ohio, and later became a franchise partner.

---

* Curtis Elder passed in 2014. Curt devoted over 30 years of his life to Donatos and poured his heart and soul into his work and life. His humor brought a smile to everyone that had the pleasure of knowing him. Curt held a number of roles at Donatos and touched many lives. He was a Father, Son, Boss, Friend, Husband, Adventurer, but most of all, a Hero. His spirit will live on in our hearts, forever.

My cousin, Matt Baumann, along with my mother at our 25ᵗʰ anniversary celebration.

In 1992 we started franchising. We also moved our home office to Gahanna, Ohio, and built a commissary in order to maintain the consistency of our product.

This was a big investment in the future growth of our company. We started our own distribution company to deliver the product to the restaurants. We had the good fortune of hiring Richard (Dick) Hill who retired from Wendy's. Dick's influence on our business set the strategy for expansion with a focused approach. He helped us make the right decisions for the distribution of our product and focus 'solely' on what we do best, make great consistent pizza. My father always believed in reinvesting in the business and not creating 'corporate' overhead. However, in order to expand the business beyond Central Ohio we knew we needed an office space that represented the quality of the business.

Dick Hill along with Dad at the ground breaking for Donatos' new office.

While our goal has always been about growing a principle-centered business, we were aware that we would only be able to grow so far as a private, family owned and operated business. So we decided the best way to grow and keep our principles alive would be to allow other like-minded people to invest in our system. We were confident we could attract principle-centered people to help us grow Donatos and have a good thing on every block. We decided to grow by franchising. We had the system and training manuals in place to ensure our people were set up for success and could make the best pizza. They were putting our name on their building and we had to trust that they were going to serve the same pizza. And trust, more importantly, that they would treat their people the way that we would treat our people. That was hard, like giving up your child, but under my brother Tom's leadership we hired Kevin King who had experience with a large pizza company and was a high school friend. Kevin led our efforts in developing the Uniform Franchise Circular. We identified the kind of people we wanted to be in business with and began franchising in the

1990s. We sold our first franchise to Tom* and
Sandy Riehl in Zanesville. Tom did a lot of the
construction and development for Donatos up until
the point that he became a franchise partner. He
was a man who exemplified the values of Donatos.
While he was 6' 10", he was larger than life itself.
His energy was contagious.

*My parents, along with Tom and Sandy Riehl and
Kevin King, our past VP of Development.*

---

* Tom Riehl passed away in 1994. Tom dedicated much of his career
to Donatos working maintenance and repairs. He was also our first
franchise partner in Zanesville, Ohio, in 1991. He is missed.

While we were growing it became obvious to us that Pizza Hut and other large pizza companies had Donatos on their radar. In 1996, not long after we introduced the edge-to-edge concept, we discovered that Pizza Hut was beginning to advertise a pizza called "The Edge." Although we are not a litigious company we knew we had to defend our trademark. Having the largest pizza company copy our product was flattering but had we not defended our brand it would have been detrimental to the future of our family business. I remember the phone call I received at home while I was on maternity leave with my daughter, Brianna. The decision to move forward in a litigious way was not a light hearted matter. We believe in protecting our brand by promoting goodwill.

Our attorney, Chuck Kegler, sent Pizza Hut a cease-and-desist letter, which Pizza Hut politely declined to do. So we brought our case in front of a judge in Franklin County, Ohio, where subpoenaed documents referenced Donatos' "edge-to-edge" language. We won a $5 million settlement for copyright infringement. This was an opportunity to invest in our systems, so we used the money from Pizza Hut to buy dough-proofing cabinets for every Donatos store.

CHUCK KEGLER
Director and Chair of
Corporate Practice, Kegler,
Brown, Hill & Ritter–*"The Edge"*

In the fall of 1997, Pizza Hut announced that it intended to introduce a new line of pizza products it was going to refer to as The Edge. We believed their proposed brand was essentially identical to and confusedly similar to Donatos' Edge to Edge® brand.

Jim Grote was reluctant to ever resort to a lawsuit to resolve what he considered to be a business dispute. But when Pizza Hut refused our request to meet with us, Jim approved our recommendation to immediately file suit in Columbus on Donatos' behalf seeking a court order restraining Pizza Hut from proceeding.

At the injunction hearing, our lead trial lawyer, Tom Hill, presented to the court in his closing argument what Jim Grote so strongly believed: *"This case is not about Pizza Hut using a thinner* crust; it isn't about putting their toppings all over the top of the pizza; it is not about cutting their pizza into squares. They can do all that stuff. And if they had done it and called their pizza 'Rim to Rim,' we wouldn't be here today. What they cannot do is steal our Edge to Edge mark and brand. That is precisely what they're trying to do."

After hearing the evidence, the Court agreed with Jim Grote, the Grote family and their Donatos associates, and granted Donatos' request enjoining Pizza Hut from referring to their new pizza as "The Edge."

After the Court's decision, the CEO of Pizza Hut flew to Columbus to meet with Jim and together they did what Jim wanted them to do before Donatos was forced to file a lawsuit: fashion a business solution satisfactory to both parties. And, in a few hours they did exactly that: fashion a business solution satisfactory to both parties.

KEVIN SNYDER
**District Supervisor,
Donatos Pizza –**
Welcome to my store

*"The first time I met Jane Abell was in 2004.
I was Pizza Hut's Director of Operations for their
Ohio based stores. Pizza Hut was very interested
in the Donatos product and I was given the
assignment to take the Pizza Hut President,
the COO, and the Head of Marketing to visit a
Donatos store. I chose the one at Mill Run.*

*As we were sitting in the Mill Run store I
noticed Jane Abell, Jim Grote, and I think Tom
Krouse in the kitchen area. Jane recognized the
Pizza Hut president and, in a perfect example of
goodwill, came over to welcome everyone to her
store, shaking hands with the biggest smile on
her face."*

Judge Blocks Pizza Hut's Ads for Its Latest Product

By a WALL STREET JOURNAL Staff Reporter

COLUMBUS, Ohio—A federal district judge temporarily took the edge off Pizza Hut's latest product.

Agreeing with a local pizza chain that Pizza Hut's new pizza, called "the Edge," could substantially hurt its business, the judge issued a temporary restraining order blocking advertising of the new product for 10 days in five Midwestern markets.

The order was sought by **Donatos Pizza** Inc. of Columbus, which contended that Pizza Hut's use of the word "edge" was likely to confuse customers familiar with Donatos's "Edge-to-Edge" pizza. Both companies' pizzas feature toppings that cover the entire pie and lack the traditional balloon-tire outer crust.

The restraining order prevents Pizza Hut from advertising its pie — though it can still sell it — in Columbus, Cincinnati and Dayton, Ohio, as well as in Indianapolis and Lexington, Ky. Officials of Pizza Hut, a unit of **Tricon Global Restaurants** Inc., couldn't be reached for comment.

Reprinted with permission of the Wall Street Journal Copyright © 1997 Dow Jones & Company, Inc. All Rights Reserved Worldwide. License number 366040412550

UNDER THE ARCHES

By 1999 we had grown to 145 stores in seven new markets. We started talking about how we were going to take Donatos to additional markets. As a family owned business we agreed that franchising was the best opportunity for growth, but it would be at a slower growth rate. At that time (1999) 80 percent of our stores were company owned.

While we wanted to grow, we knew we had options. We could go public, seek out private equity financing, angel investors, co-brand and other opportunities that would infuse capital. We explored all of these alternatives. I think the most important thing to us in guiding our thinking was our principles and fulfilling my dad's vision to "be a principle based business on every block around the world."

Our Vision is to be a principle based company dedicated to the best products, developing the best people, built to last for 100 years and beyond. We really believe in my father's purpose for going into business originally, which was to create an environment around every restaurant where we could make a difference; where we could promote

Chapter 1: **A REALLY GOOD PRODUCT**

goodwill in the community, be a good neighbor and live our principles.

Whether we decided to go public, or find alternative ways to grow, we were going to grow the business based on the Golden Rule, to treat others the way you want to be treated. That was the goal, but more importantly we would only grow if we could keep our heart and soul. It is our "soul" reason for being in business. Then in 1999 McDonald's came knocking on our door.

We had been in conversations with another well known hamburger chain based out of Columbus about co-branding. So the fact that McDonald's called us to meet with them piqued our curiosity. McDonald's was pursuing a Meal Occasion Strategy where they would acquire other concepts in the industry. We were not exactly sure what to think when they sent their private plane to have us visit their headquarters in Chicago. Did they want to co-brand, invest as a minority partner or buy the family business?

They told us that they searched all over the world looking for The Best in Class. They said they had been in every one of our restaurants and they believed we had Best in Class Pizza and Best in Class People. They were looking to diversify their brand portfolio.

And we were told that out of over 60 different pizza companies they were reviewing, we were identified as the best in the class.

TOM KROUSE
**President and CEO,
Donatos Pizza–*A meal
occasion strategy***

"I think that McDonald's decided to experiment with its approach to expansion because they had reached the point that they believed they couldn't just keep building more restaurants and growing same-store sales. They started looking at buying other businesses that could complement their business, not compete with it.

From this line of thinking came their 'meal occasion strategy.' McDonald's wanted to own the entire stomach of the American people–from hamburgers to pizza to chicken to Mexican food. So they decided to go looking for the 'best in class' companies in these categories. And that's what brought them to Donatos.

They targeted companies in varying stages of maturity, such as Chipotle, which was new and emerging, and Boston Market, which was big, but struggling. Donatos was considered strong and established, but a smaller player in an important category. They looked at 63 pizza chains around the world and chose Donatos for the quality of the product, the culture, and the top-drawer people that made up the company."

McDONALD'S—NOT AN EXIT STRATEGY

I think many people might say that starting a business, growing it, being acquired by the world's largest restaurant company, and then finally having the money to do something else, take money off the table and/or retire, would be their goal. But, it was never my father's goal. Our goal was to continue to grow the company so we could promote goodwill.

The thought of selling our family business was overwhelming. Here we were a family owned and operated business based on the philosophy that putting the money back in the business fuels the growth, faced with a decision to sell 100 percent of our company. While we weighed all of the pros and cons to selling the business, not one of our family members mentioned what it would mean to them financially. My dad and mom had great estate advice and we were all owners of the business.

It was a hard decision mostly because we were talking about growth, but we really weren't talking about selling the whole company. We really weren't talking about selling anything. A lot of mergers and acquisitions were going on in the late 90s and a lot of companies were trying to figure out how to get more of a share of peoples' stomachs.

But we still did not expect McDonald's to offer to buy the whole thing. My dad, my brother and I flew to Chicago and met with Jack Greenberg, CEO of McDonald's. My brother with his global vision immediately saw the opportunities this would provide for our people and our franchise partners.

Selling the company would certainly infuse enough capital to help us fulfill the vision to grow around the world. My dad and I were still taking in the idea of selling the family business and a little slower to show any excitement.

I remember while we (family) were deciding on whether to sell my dad said, "We have an opportunity to grow our business and prove that you can build a business and keep your principles." So we weighed the pros and cons of each option. We knew we needed to do something different to grow the business beyond what we were doing. We were excited about what we could learn from the world's largest restaurant company and knew they had the intellectual capital to help us grow the business.

Our family strategized for three months with the help of the smartest people in their fields: Chuck Kegler (legal), Ted McClellan (real estate) and Jim Wyland (financing and wealth management) along with our internal team, my brother Tom Grote COO, Mike Sosinski CFO (now a franchise partner) and Kevin King Senior VP of Development (now a valued alumnus).

JIM WYLAND
Founder and Managing Partner, WealthStone

"Since 1989, attorney Chuck Kegler and I have advised the family on legal matters, business strategy, financing and wealth management. We're basically tasked with telling them the truth, helping them leverage what they've got, and giving them strategic advice all along the way.

Jim was very particular about building his inner circle, but he was smart enough to know he needed a team of trusted advisors to help him avoid the mistakes that are common in a family business, even a successful one. The key to success in this inner circle is trust, of course. But you also have to like each other. Everyone involved really needs to know what they are doing, be an excellent listener, and have a keen sense of the strengths and weaknesses of everyone involved.

While each member of the Grote family is very different from the other, they share the same values and are all very focused and fairly objective, which makes them very good at considering alternatives and understanding their options as a group.

One of many things I've learned from Jim Grote is how smart it is to be generous. He lives the win-win. He has a knack, a truly unique entrepreneurial sensibility. Any time he's had the chance to do more or give back, he's done it."

Dad during the McDonald's days.

While it wasn't the goal, selling to McDonald's somehow not only provided the financial freedom, but the emotional freedom to the family. While we didn't realize it, the internal responsibility of staying in the family business was lifted. For the first time I believe our family felt the emotional freedom to do something completely different with our lives. Growing up in a family business, even if you're working somewhere else, you still have the feeling like that's the legacy you're supposed to carry on. There is an emotional connection that is difficult to explain until you are free from the identity of the business.

We had a lot of pros and a couple of cons to selling the business. The cons were linked to the culture of McDonald's and how it may be different from our family's principles. We questioned how we were going to continue to grow the company with the same soul and spirit of our family business. If we sold to McDonald's, the family would agree to stay on board. But ultimately we found that not all of us wanted to work for a different company under the same name of Donatos.

While we were in due diligence, we wanted to ensure that their culture was based in a strong spirit of people first and servant leadership. As the Chief People Officer for Donatos, I had the opportunity to interview key leaders at the company and found that they had a culture of promoting from within and their culture, although different from ours, was deep and rich in tradition. I met some of the most incredible people during my journey.

I was inspired with the talent, the passion and the leaders in their Human Resources Department. I remember meeting Steve Russell (McDonald's) and

Bob Wilner (Chipotle) who reinforced through their actions and leadership that the Human Resource Department shouldn't be a policy-making department. It should be a people development department. They have continued to be two individuals that I admire and aspire to emulate.

Communicating the decision to sell was going to be difficult but rewarding. A huge pro for selling was what we could do for our people, those who were part of our Donatos family. Selling the family business meant growth opportunity and development for the people who built Donatos. We felt a sense of responsibility to these people. With the sale we were able to give to the people who worked so hard for Donatos a special payment as a "Thank You". These were the people that dedicated their lives to the family business.

All of our managers received one week pay for every year they had been with our company. We attended a Cincinnati Reds game and my brother stood up on a chair, right in the middle of the crowd, and one by one handed out checks. Forty weeks, 25 weeks, 30 weeks. It was a great way of giving back to the people who poured their hearts and souls into the company. In addition, we were able to pay out our Stock

Taunya Eckhardt* and Cindy Jackson receiving checks from the company at the Cincinnati Reds game.

Appreciation Rights (SARs) to the Executive Team. Because we were a privately owned company we designed a phantom stock plan for the leadership in order to recruit and retain the best people. This event triggered a pay out to the team. Basically they all received an early retirement package. That was a great day!

Communicating to the franchise partners was a bit more difficult. Our franchise partners signed a 20-year agreement to be in business with our family. They invested their hard earned money into a concept and a business led by the family. And all of a sudden they

---

* Tragically we lost Taunya in 2006 at age 42. She'll always hold a special place in my heart.

were in business with someone else, McDonald's. While the sale gave our franchise partners the opportunity to grow, and some were very excited about the future, they were a little skeptical of the new relationship.

My brother Tom stayed for two years as COO. He led the efforts for growth and expansion but most importantly the execution of our mission and promise. After a few years, he decided to gain the experience of opening a brand new market. Tom moved to Philadelphia and opened 11 stores in 12 months. Tom went back to school. He got his master's degree from Wharton School of Business, graduating in the top 10 percent of his class. He's brilliant. During that time things were changing fast. The dynamics of a corporate culture were infiltrating the company.

I think deep in Tom's heart he knew that he wanted to help build the business; he knew he could do it. But he wanted to do something on his own. He is an entrepreneur and working for a big corporation created internal conflict. That's when Tom opened a restaurant called *Out on Main* in Columbus, Ohio. Now he is an owner and the CFO of Green Biologics, a biofuel company based in London, England. He also helped found Equity Ohio, a charitable organization focused on LGBT equality. He has a husband, Rick Neal, and two adopted children, Amoret and Sophia.

My sister Katie stayed for a year and led our catering efforts and expansion into new markets. She's a free spirit and after a couple of years into the corporate structure she decided to leave. I was living in fear myself at the time, and could tell it just wasn't something she wanted to do. Previously, she had opened her own coffee and video store and, always creative, Katie is now a freelance artist living in Florida with her life partner and best friend Bob Sawyer, their three daughters and grandchildren.

Kyle, my younger brother, happened on a self-exploration journey to Colorado, just for a visit, and found himself surrounded by people with the same passion for organic and naturally grown foods. So he attended a land auction of 2,800 acres that had the largest artisian water supply in the area. And my younger free-spirited brother bought the whole farm. He is living and working on his ranch with over 300 Yak, free range chickens, and a Yak and Cracker Farm to Table store. He's working harder than he has ever worked in his entire life. He has a wife, Teanna, and two children, Soraya and Elijah.

TOM GROTE
Jane's Older Brother—
I loved the business

"I had all kinds of jobs at Donatos when I was growing up. I really enjoyed working for the company; I loved the business, the people and the challenges. After I graduated my dad and I talked about whether I should go work for another company to gain some outside experience. But Donatos had a need at the time and I already knew the business very well. By the time McDonald's bought the company, I had been the #2 at Donatos for several years.

I think most people, including myself, expected that I would grow into the #1 role in the company. What's interesting to me now is realizing that I discovered my value as the #2 man in my years with Donatos. I didn't know it at the time, but later when I was running my own company, I became very aware of my strength as the #2 guy. I'm good at that.

My value to Donatos, I think, was in strategic planning and establishing some process and protocols that made a big difference in the business right away. It was a very productive period for Donatos, but not without its challenges!

The McDonald's environment didn't suit me. I went to Philadelphia to help open that market, then took a leave of absence to go to Wharton for my MBA and figure out what I wanted to do. Leaving the company was the right thing for me at the time because I realized there were others who could do what I was doing for the company.

Jane was different, though. I thought what she was doing for the company was something only she could do. I pushed her to step up and speak up, which made her uncomfortable. I literally had to push her on to the stage during the McDonald's years, but it was an important part of her development. It caused her to grow into the confident leader she is today."

KATIE GROTE
Jane's Younger Sister—*Dad has always been proud of his children*

"Being raised in an entrepreneurial environment made us kids a little fearless in our own ways. Donatos was all we knew. Selling to McDonald's made me think for the first time, 'Is this what I want to do?'

I studied art in college, but didn't have the confidence to pursue it as a career. I was confident in business, having worked for Donatos. They moved me around, hoping I would discover a spot where I would feel a passion for my work. I was attracted to Catering because it was like a small company inside a company. It was growing fast, and catering to large groups and gatherings was exciting and fun.

What I liked best about my work then was collaborating with other people to figure things out, to find solutions. I loved hashing things out, even when it was rough, because we'd always come back to the core of what Donatos meant, what it stood for.

McDonald's created a door for me to walk through that would allow me to get on with my own life. It wasn't easy to step through that door, however. I didn't want to leave the people behind. Leaving felt like I was leaving family, some people I have known for most of my life.

The CEO, Bill Rose, sent me to a leadership conference. He was nudging me to commit to the company. The conference was incredible, but it had exactly the opposite effect on me. I came to the realization that I had other passions in life. I needed to leave the company to fully explore it.

It was very difficult for me to tell my dad that I was leaving. All my life he had encouraged me to do what I wanted.

When I finally told him, he was great about it. My dad has always been proud of his children and a great source of strength and support.

Today I am doing art, painting and sculpting, and in the future will be doing readings for people. Moving away helped, I could start fresh, take bold steps, and explore my talents."

KYLE GROTE
Jane's Younger Brother—
They are all my heros

"I started working in the commissary, because Dad said it was important to earn your own money. I also worked in the stores, folding boxes and cleaning pans. Then I worked in the home office as a marketing analyst for a short period.

When growing up, my dad would always tell us to do the right thing so you don't ever have to look over your shoulder. He taught me to do business in a win-win way: If it's good for you but not good for the person you're doing business with, it's not worth it.

Now that I'm running a ranch, I call on those kinds of principles every day. My dad has had that influence on every member of my family. I've watched them work so hard and do such amazing things–they are all my heroes."

As I stated earlier, entrepreneur-ism runs deep in our family and didn't stop short with my mom and her side of the family. She was one of two women in her family who was told that she would just be wasting her money if she went to college because she was a woman. So she put college off until later in life to help my dad with the business.

My mom left Donatos shortly before the sale to McDonald's to pursue her own journey of entrepreneur-ism. She is an exceptionally smart woman who has the ability to balance compassion with creativity. She has a thirst for knowledge and recently graduated with her second master's degree in clinical behavior psychology. Previously she owned and operated her own business–Gentle Wind, consisting of five retail outlets. Her mission is to help people with self discovery.

I believe there is a difference between entrepreneurs and entrepreneurial spirit. Entrepreneurs will risk everything to start something that has their identity associated with it. I believe I have more of an entrepreneurial spirit–someone who will risk a lot and have the passion to carry the torch but it doesn't necessarily represent my own identity. I have never had a desire to go out and build something on my own.

I'm the only one out of the whole family that didn't start something on my own. But I am proud to carry the torch–the legacy of the company–with passion.

KEY LEARNINGS

Looking back, 1999 ended up being a great year to sell our business. There were a number of public companies acquiring other concepts in the restaurant industry. We were fortunate that we were a very profitable company and we sold for a multiple of earnings that included the intangibles like goodwill.

During the four years we were with McDonald's, we built 75 new stores in three new markets and one new country. We opened four restaurants in Munich, Germany. It was a great experience for me. I was learning a lot about real estate, franchising, marketing, training and people development. I also learned about the McDonald's culture and how to put processes in place. All in all, it was a wonderful opportunity. But it was also a learning experience about what not to do.

McDonald's is an incredible organization made up of great people and great systems. They operate like a manufacturing company within the restaurants. Even though we had already developed a drive-up window for the pizza industry, McDonald's taught us how to be efficient. We learned a tremendous amount. And as was our goal, our business began to grow, but so did our expenses. Under the direction of McDonald's, our administrative costs went from our previous level of $10 million to $28 million in one year. We hired 23 new Vice Presidents and moved into a new Home Office doubling the size of our administrative staff and overhead expense.

This was an important time because we were merging three different cultures: McDonald's, other outside executives and Donatos people. During the due diligence and shortly after we sold the company, I went on maternity leave with my third child, Tori. She surprised me by arriving three weeks early, on Christmas Eve. I went back to work after four weeks of maternity leave and found myself all of a sudden walking around introducing myself to new people. My first order of business from our new CEO was to hire a Chief Marketing Officer. He was the last hire to complete the newly formed Executive Team. I hired Tom Krouse who came highly recommended by a lot of people in the industry. He was the Vice President of Marketing at Wendy's.

Coming back after being off with my three kids was difficult, having just sold the company, going on maternity leave, and coming back to so many "new" people and a new boss. I felt responsible for the culture as the Chief People Officer. I failed at ensuring that we had the right on-boarding experience. I will never forget the first conversation I had with my new boss, our new CEO. During the due diligence, we never discussed having a new CEO for the company. My father had been the only other CEO in our family business, except for a short time when my uncle Ron Zeller joined the company and later left to pursue his interest in another family owned and operated restaurant.

McDonald's taught us a lot about real estate, people development and franchising. When you look for real estate sites it is an art and a science. The demographics are critical to the success of the restaurant–the traffic control, right side of the road, household head count, etc. But, you also have to make sure that the restaurant fits the neighborhood, that there's the right "chemistry." Even if a site appears to be an "A" site, it still may not be a good site for us.

It's the same with people balancing art and science. People with experience may not be the "right" people.

Even if the resume looks great you still have to have the "chemistry." It's not the "right fit" if their values are not aligned. People have to be willing to learn to work in a new environment. And to do that, you have to like the people you work with. You really have to love what you do. If you don't, it won't be a happy environment.

I'm very passionate about the "chemistry", the fit, and having a happy environment, what is often called culture. I believe that culture is living and breathing in a company. It changes depending on experiences, and it changes all the time, just like families do. Families will go through marriages, babies, divorces and death but the heart and the soul of the family is always based on a common core of value. This creates a "soul" or a "spirit" of the family. Like families, the culture of a company can change, but it is important to keep the soul and the spirit alive.

Soon after the acquisition, Dad held the title as Chairman, and McDonald's named a new CEO. When the new CEO started, on his first day, I decided as Chief People Officer (and keeper of the culture) to share with him that he needed to start his on-boarding process by going to work in the stores. I told him how important it was to our culture and I gave him his Donatos shirts. He looked at me, and he was really a good guy, but he said that he was the CEO and he didn't have time to work in the stores.

I remember that day clearly as I pushed the shirts back across the table and said, "You're not going to be CEO unless you fulfill our mission and promise." You could have heard a pin drop in that room that day as he looked at me and said, "I don't think you understand, I am going to be the CEO," and he got up and walked out of the room. I looked at my brother and my dad and realized that this was going to be a different mode of operation.

Since I had only worked for Donatos, and directly for my family, I was used to having the freedom to express my opinions. This was going to be a good learning experience for me, but I honestly was kind of taken back. He looked at me like he wanted to pat me on the head and say "oh honey, you're not going to make it." I remember walking out of the office thinking this is going to be different but I'm not going to change who I am. Little did I know that in the months to follow I would lose my soul in this new and different work environment.

Immediately following the acquisition, the newly formed team began to work on "our concept". I remember Fred Turner, Senior Chairman of the Board for McDonald's at the time they bought Donatos, coming to our office. He said to my dad, "Whatever you do, don't let us mess up your company." We all laughed at the time, but I think Fred wanted us to know that they bought us because we were best in class for pizza and not to lose our soul. Months following, we developed a process called the Consumer Driven Feedback Process (CDFP) to gain insights from customers on what our brand should look like going forward. We had a great team of experts on leading the process. Scott Zuckerman from McDonald's and Dave Muenz from Proctor & Gamble led the initiative. The idea was to build a new concept with the same great pizza.

The CDFP process was a great way to truly understand our business from the customers' perspective. The team led a number of focus-groups; we built mock up kitchens, re-wrote our manuals and all of our back of the house procedures. The new concept was designed to capture the dine-in business for pizza. Many pizza companies had walked away from building buildings to accommodate a dining experience.

We completely changed our model from 70 percent off-premise to 70 percent on-premise. This changed the type of people we had to hire, the way the kitchens were set up and the delivery of our pizza. This also significantly changed our financial model. Our Sales to Investment Ratio was no longer attractive. But we kept building buildings, faster than we were able to develop our people.

PUBLIC VERSUS PRIVATE

Based on my experience, the difference between the way a Public company operates and a Private company operates was quite insightful.

I obviously understood the difference between public and private on paper. Reading business cases in business class was totally different from experiencing it firsthand. Working with a public company helped me recognize the difference in how decisions are made. While being a publicly held company isn't bad, we found ourselves making very short-term business decisions because we had to react to "the market." Here we were, this little pizza company inside the world's largest restaurant company, and yet our decisions had to be based on the Quarterly Earnings and Wall Street's expectations.

One of my earliest experiences came when the decision was made to close an entire market (Atlanta), all 23 stores, and yet 50 percent of them were making money. The decision was made to close the entire market by the end of the quarter in order to take a write-off.

Our CEO would hold a meeting and lead us down a path to arrive at the pre-determined outcome. We would spend hours reviewing the business case to keep the market open or close it. All the while, the decision had already been made to close the market. Once we came to the decision that was in alignment with the CEO we were able to move forward and put a plan together.

This was a perfect example of how the "street" influenced short-term business decisions. After the meeting, I went to speak to Bill about the decision and asked for clarification. He agreed that it was a short-term decision. While we were investing in growth, McDonald's was starting to receive a lot of criticism about taking their eye off their their core business. So we had to send a message to the street (Wall Street) and it had to be now, good or bad, that we were serious about profits.

It was a great learning experience for me, living and making decisions about your business on a quarterly basis.

As a family business, we had always invested in the long term, what we call our prosperity. For me, I think living the difference between a family business and a public corporation was important. It was also the first time we ever had to close a significant number of restaurants, which meant we would be effecting a number of people's lives.

After the meeting with Bill Rose, our CEO, I went back to my office and reflected on the outcome. Since we couldn't control the circumstances and the decision, at least we could control how we were going to close the restaurants. We put together a team of people and everyone agreed, if we're going to do this we're going to do it with our Mission in place. Our goal was to have every manager have a new job by the end of the two weeks. We're going to give them notice before we close the stores. Every hourly associate will get a severance package. We would do it with Goodwill.

CULTURE HAS TO HAVE A PROCESS

It seems like one of those simple things. It was important for me to be true to my principles as I continued down this new path. Closing a market and impacting over 300 people's careers took its toll on me.

After a few meetings with our CEO I began doubting myself, questioning my abilities and I lost focus. I had a couple of situations where I was put in my place publicly. I was humiliated. I started working from a place of my own self worth instead of for the mission of the company. I started working in fear.

The funny thing about fear is that you start working harder and longer with less clarity. Here I was, our Chief People Officer (CPO), and our culture was important to me and I was living in fear. I talked about it all the time to our managers. I had never had to work in a place where the Mission was just something that hung on the wall. It reminded me that in order to keep a strong culture we had to have a process. It doesn't just happen because you have good people who care about making it happen.

We take great care in making our pizza so that our customers can get that same pizza every single time. It's our contract with our customers—every time it's the same high quality product. We took so much time and attention in our pizza process, but we didn't take that same time and attention with our people. Culture is our "contract" with our people. It, too, has to have a process.

A process can sound restrictive as it relates to people but there are some important systems that have to be in place to keep the spirit alive:

- ✓ Hire the "right" people, those whose values "fit", using tools that measure values
- ✓ Measure results by setting goals (Performance Management System)
- ✓ Succession planning should be based on principles and results and reviewed at every level in the organization
- ✓ Compassionate accountability with a feedback process
- ✓ Training people is different than development and you have to do both for the person to fully develop into the best skilled leader

Values are not the "soft stuff," something that people shouldn't talk about. You should talk about them all the time, so much so that people are tired of hearing about your values. This is part of the lessons I learned working as the CPO for Donatos under the arches. You can never take your culture for granted. It requires constant attention to details.

TOM SANTOR
**Executive Director of Public
Relations**–*Culture under the arches*

*"I think that all of us at Donatos learned a lot during
the McDonald's years. The people that I got to work
with were incredibly professional and knowledgeable
as well as being genuinely wonderful people. They
had fantastic systems and incredible resources...
far beyond what we had at our disposal.*

*But for all the synergies, there were lots of
dichotomies as well. Their business centered
on dining in and driving through, our business
centered on delivery and carry out. They were
busiest at breakfast and lunch, we're all about
dinner and late night. Their business was partial
to good weather, whereas the pizza business
thrives on inclement weather.*

*Our business personality is very forthcoming and
people-driven, whereas theirs was (understandably
so) more guarded and company-driven. Simply two
different cultures operating under one roof."*

BUSINESS INTUITION VS. BUSINESS CASES

I also learned a lot from McDonald's about business intuition and building a "business case." My dad is a true entrepreneur. I have an entrepreneurial "spirit" and McDonald's is very business focused. They have a lot of very smart people, lots of people with degrees. They are incredibly talented people. They relied heavily on focus groups, agencies and business cases to gather the facts. All of this seems important, but so different for an entrepreneur who built a business on intuition and a good gut instinct.

Looking back, I would say if I had to pick between the two approaches, I'd put more of the emphasis on the entrepreneur's intuition. Business cases are important, but there are many times when the decisions were not in alignment with intuition. Entrepreneurial spirit with a balance of business case is critical in building and sustaining a business.

SURROUND YOURSELF WITH PEOPLE SMARTER THAN YOURSELF.

A SIMPLE TRUTH FROM THE BOOK GOOD TO GREAT BY JIM COLLINS.

There were lots of good people at McDonald's, but there are two people in their company that stood out to me. Steve Russell was their Senior Vice President of Human Resources. He was very influential and encouraged me to stay true to myself.

The other individual in Human Resources was Bob Wilner. Most of my time with Bob was when we had to do our first rightsizing. We had never had to lay people off in our 40 year history, nor had McDonald's. Bob later went on to join Chipotle and has recently retired and started a consulting business. Steve has since retired from McDonald's. Both of these individuals taught me that it is possible to have a (People Focused) People Department that is about people in a large company.

Downsizing is a difficult thing to do when you are impacting people's lives and trying to maintain a culture of trust. It was important for people to understand "why" we were making the decisions and what it meant to them personally. Since we had never had to lay people off, I started researching the best way to downsize and keep a healthy culture. This led me to a process that we still use to this day for succession planning.

We started with a blank sheet of paper and began by identifying all of the essential roles and responsibilities needed to fulfill Our Mission. Once we identified the "white boxes" without names, we went to work on putting people back in the organization. This was important, because it allowed us to take an objective look at the roles and make sure that we had the right people on the bus in the right seats. In order to determine which people should be put back into the organization we ranked them on their Core Principles first and then Results.

I enjoyed my experience with McDonald's. It gave me an opportunity to work for another company without having to leave Donatos. I learned a lot from them, but most of all I learned a lot about myself, as a person. It began with my learning to take risks that are outside of my comfort zone. I learned that negative people take the energy out of me. I have always believed a statement that my Uncle Jim Baumann made to my father early in life, "be careful while you are in business, you can take away someone's job but never take away their dignity and respect". That one quote became the guardrails for how we treat people when they make mistakes or when they have to become alumni. Everyone deserves to be treated with dignity and respect.

I value the fact that I was able to work in fear. This taught me a valuable lesson. Good people can fall into the fear trap. I learned the "shadow of a leader" is long. The wrong leader can create an undercurrent of fear throughout an organization. It reinforced my belief to do the right thing, always. And it all made me realize how much I really loved our business and our people. And it was my love of the business coupled with the principles I brought to work every day–Character, Courage, Conviction and Compassion–that led to the biggest thing I learned. We needed to buy our company back from McDonald's.

BUYBACK DECISION

In 2003 McDonald's stock hit a historic low and rumor hit the streets that they were going to spin off, sell or close all of their other brands and focus on hamburgers. As soon as the rumor hit, my dad walked into my office. I was excited and when he sat down I immediately laid out an idea for buying the company back from McDonald's. I stated that I would sell everything I had, put all my money back into it but I needed his leadership and, well honestly, I needed his money.

From February to October 2003 no one knew what was going to happen. Many people were just concerned for their own family's well being. Our store managers were not as concerned, which is amazing to me, and I want to say they were protected but they weren't. They heard the rumors. Our VP of Operations was trying to help people by telling them to go find other employment, but it was actually creating a bit of fear in the company.

JIM WYLAND
Founder and Managing Partner, WealthStone—*Buying the company back*

"In the early fall of 2003, McDonald's former CEO came back to the company to get their stock back up and bring the focus back on their core business, which meant unloading the brands they had acquired, including Donatos. Jane lit up at the thought of buying back the company. She insisted that we had to do this. She said we'd learned things and could bring the business back to

what it was and be even better than before. She convinced her dad to do it with her.

It was interesting to walk through the process of evaluating the company and negotiating the price and terms to buy it back. Donatos now had a lot of issues it had never had before. McDonald's had brought in expensive executives. Overhead had swelled and some bad real estate decisions had been made when opening new markets. Chuck Kegler did a great job of negotiating for Donatos.

The buyback was great, very exciting. But Jane and Jim had their hands full bringing the company back to what it was. The culture had become very frayed and the entrepreneurial spirit of the company had gone into hibernation during the McDonald's years. But Jane was all in. She put everything she had back into the company and put all of her passion behind setting things right."

There were people who would come to us and say, "I felt like I cheated on a company but I interviewed with someone else." For months, that was going on. One-by-one the leadership team had to make decisions that were best for their families. This was an important time for our company.

Since all the affiliate brands with McDonald's were being dismantled, we had multi-concept human resource round tables for best practices. During these discussions retention bonuses were recommended. I was never a fan of retention bonuses. I believed if we were honest with people about our intentions we would not have to incentivize people to stay. We wanted people to stay because they wanted to be at Donatos, not because they were getting an extra bonus to stay.

McDonald's put together a team to evaluate the options of either closing Donatos and selling the real estate or selling Donatos altogether. Meanwhile, there were a few of us looking at how to buy Donatos back. Tom Krouse was in this inner circle. Although with respect to Tom, he didn't know if he was going to have a job either. In all those organizational scenarios we created, he would come back and say he's interviewing just in case he had to find another job.

I remember every single thing about the day we went to McDonald's to present our plan. I remember what I wore. I remember being at the airport. At times like that, you can remember the smells. I remember on that day it was crisp, it was clean, it was October and fall is my favorite time of the year. I remember going to the airport. I remember what the driver was like taking us to McDonald's.

On the family side, my dad was in attendance with Tom Krouse and me. On the Plan B—Close and Sell side it was our CFO and a few other McDonald's people. We all flew together because at that point we're all Donatos. Although emotions were high and adrenaline was rushing, it was a business deal that we were up against. It was a business deal for McDonald's and we respected that they were interested in getting some of their money back.

The CFO was going to present the plan to close Donatos, or sell it to private equity. It was a transaction. That was part of respecting that it was a business transaction and he's doing his job. McDonald's paid him to make sure he looked at it objectively enough to determine what they should do with our family business. That was fair.

CHUCK KEGLER
Director and Chair of Corporate Practice, Kegler, Brown, Hill & Ritter—*"It must be fair."*

"In 1999, we represented Jim, Jane & the Grote Family in the sale of Donatos to McDonald's. Our firm continued to represent Donatos and McDonald's during the four years of McDonald's' ownership. Because of the urgency of completing the divestiture by year-end, and our familiarity with the Donatos' restaurants, McDonald's consented to allow our firm to represent Jim and Jane in their negotiations with McDonald's.

Those six or seven months structuring and negotiating a plan to purchase Donatos were exhilarating—a lot of work, but fun. Jane was very excited about the potential, to again partner with her Donatos' associates and she pushed hard to keep the process moving forward. It was a stressful and difficult time for Donatos' people because of the uncertainty of what was happening and what could happen.

During the repurchase negotiations, McDonald's business people and their lawyers were tough but fair. However, McDonald's made one business request that Jim believed was not fair to Jim, Jane, and their Donatos' associates. The point was negotiated in McDonald's' home office over the course of the final several days of negotiation. On the last day of negotiations, we spent almost the entire day talking about this last business issue. Late in the day, when both sides were tired, frustrated and hungry, Jim suggested we excuse ourselves and go to another conference room to discuss with Jim whether he was being unreasonable in refusing to agree to McDonald's' final demand. As we brainstormed alternatives, we walked around in a smoked glass conference room in McDonald's offices. Through the glass, McDonald's could see that we were walking around and writing on a white board, but could not see what we were writing or hear what we were saying. Several times McDonald's' counsel tried to interrupt us, indicating they were not just tired and hungry but that they had some other suggestions, but Jim refused to talk any further until he fully understood the issue and was in a position to make what he believed would be a proposal that was fair for both parties.

As the evening wore on, we all became more and more tired and hungry, the CEO of McDonald's knocked on

Continued on page 114

Continued from page 113

the door and asked to speak with Jim adding 'we will wait as long as you want, but please stop writing on the white board because we give up and concede this last point to you.' Jim said 'OK–if they are willing to concede the point, my position on the issue must be fair. So let's stop talking and get this deal closed.' That scene makes us laugh to this day."

There were key people in the decision making for McDonald's. Matts Leaderhausen and Chris Catalano were in charge of the affiliated brands and they led the McDonald's Brand Board. When we first started the conversation with McDonald's, Chris and Matts were very supportive and encouraged us to buy the company back. They helped make sure it was feasible for us. They helped McDonald's see the value of the business in a buyback. And because it was a leveraged buyout, we had the opportunity to have them sit on our board for three years. These two individuals are the reason we were able to purchase the company back.

But the most important people in our decision to buy back the company were our associates. I will always remember, after buying the company back from

McDonald's, dad and I stood in front of them to tell them things were going to change. At our next banquet, Tom Krouse presented a framed picture signed by each associate. The picture is of Dad and me standing under the sign at our first Donatos store. And the saying is:

> **"We are all eternally grateful**
> **And we won't let you down."**

And they never have. ♥

Dad and me receiving a framed photo signed by our associates reading, "We are all eternally grateful and we won't let you down."

LAURA FORDING
**Assistant Controller,
Donatos Pizza—*They trust me***

"I started with Donatos in 1989 when there were 19 stores. I have always been in accounting and I have seen a lot of changes. But the one constant is the Donatos people. We are here to work and do good things for Donatos. We get close. We become friends. You immediately know everyone's name. The atmosphere allows for having fun while we do our jobs.

Donatos is passionate about people, about developing them and giving back to the community. People are treated with respect and dignity. I can just sense it, who is a Donatos' person and who isn't. It's just something you feel. We aren't doing it because we are told, but because we believe in the quality. It's amazing to me how the alumni get together. Many of us keep our old phone lists. Someone comes back in town and we meet to discuss 'old times.' People love Donatos and how they have been treated.

Our leaders convey the culture. If there is an opening in the home office, they look for people from the field (the stores). People have a lot of opportunities to thrive and grow into what they are doing. You can approach anyone, talk to anyone, people don't use their titles. It doesn't feel like there are any layers. It wasn't that way during the McDonald's years. Donatos people roll up their sleeves and everyone pitches in. When it comes to month end closing, my boss Doug Kourie asks me how he can help.

I will always remember after the buyback from McDonald's there was a $15 million dollar loan to Donatos. It is my job to watch the money. One morning when I came in the money was gone. I panicked until Jim told me he had moved it into a CD. I told him to never do that again without telling me. I was adamant. He loves telling everybody that story. It's great–they trust me with every penny they have."

THE MISSING PIECE Jane Grote Abell

.

CHAPTER 2
THE 4C's OF SUCCESS

At Donatos, there has been a deep and authentic commitment to our principles from day one. This is not due to some kind of altruism or selflessness on our part; it's simply a result of the way my dad was raised and because we have found it to be the most effective way to do business. It's not always the most convenient or inexpensive approach but in the end I can say with absolute certainty that besides our quality product, our principles have been the single most important factor in the company's passion for quality and success over a half century in business.

There are four principles that are critical to me and to the success of our company, and it starts with the people behind the brand. I refer to them as the 4C's of Success–Character, Courage, Conviction and Compassion.

CHARACTER

*"Character is like a tree and reputation like
a shadow. The shadow is what we think of it;
the tree is the real thing."*
–Abraham Lincoln

To me, character is the center of our being, our core,
our innermost thoughts and our actions when no
one is looking, when we are alone with ourselves,
truly alone and it is quiet and all you hear is your
heart beating. Your mind is thinking, and you ask
the question "who am I"?

I believe our character is reflected through our
actions. It is a reflection of our first response
to life's obstacles and successes. It is how we
immediately respond to someone when they are
hurt, when our friend receives recognition or a
promotion, when we are confronted with an angry
person, when we fail, when we succeed, and when
we are faced with a decision to act in a crisis.

Character is the fiber of our existence. I believe
our character is built through our environment

and our strength of character is built through life's experiences. I have been blessed in my life to be around people who challenged me personally and professionally and tested my strength of character. If it were not for my experiences I would not be the person that I am today.

Our families are often important sources of our values and home is the place where character begins to develop. It's true that the people you know, especially early in life, help to shape your character. But it's not just family; it can be a teacher, a spiritual mentor or a coach—even a boss that makes the difference.

My father's early experiences in business gave him the determination to be in business for himself. My father learned at the early age of 13 about how important it is to treat your employees with respect and dignity and to make sure the customers get the same quality pizza every time they order. He always believed that when a customer bought their first pizza it became an unwritten contract and they should expect the same pizza every time.

The people who help shape your character are not always the "good" people in your life. Sometimes exposure to a person with different values than your own leaves a mark, permanently coloring the way you see yourself in the world. My dad had a "character-building" experience early in his life that made a tremendous impression on him, and later in my own life.

I remember the stories of how my dad's first managers treated the people and mismanaged the product and money in the pizza shop where he worked. Dad was determined to open up a pizza shop where people could bring their principles to work with them.

I suppose these stories were forming my character in my very early years as we used to tease my dad about giving us lectures. There were so many of them that we started to number them to save him time from lecturing us. We would say, "OK–lecture 112, we know, we know... 'Always treat others the way you want to be treated,' or lecture 306, 'Do what you say you are going to do when you say you are going to do it.'"

AUTHENTICITY

One of my first lessons in life has been about authenticity. Even though I knew in my head who I was, I didn't always have the heart to live it out loud.

I used to listen to stories that potential candidates would tell me about how they were treated at work. I believe that you should be able to be the same person at work that you are at home, and the same person you are at home that you are at work. When these are not in alignment then something is wrong with the situation. I do not believe you should have to put armor on when you go to work, nor when you go home. Everyone should be able to bring their 'whole self' to work.

If you find yourself stopping and taking a deep breath before you go into work and feeling like you have to be someone you are not, then you are probably in the wrong job, or environment, and may not be living an authentic life. I believe that everyone who works at Donatos should be able to come to work and have the courage to live their values out loud.

Our time on earth is our chance to stand for something. I believe that life is more beautiful and we are stronger when we are authentic. It is about learning who you are and being true to yourself, not trying to live up to something or someone your parents, friends or co-workers expect you to be.

TRANSPARENCY

The second character trait I learned in life through my experiences in business is transparency. I don't even know that I understood what that meant until I watched my dad and mom over the years. I have never run into a person that had a negative thing to say about my mom or dad. I know it is not because they are perfect. I believe it is because they are authentic and transparent. I learned from them that it is OK to make a mistake, as long as you admit it and make changes to avoid making the same one over and over again. We are all human and we all make mistakes.

I learned that the more transparent I was with my own mistakes the more trust I would build with people. We can't expect our managers and associates to admit to a mistake on a pizza if we can't admit to our own mistakes in life. Some believe it is easier to reposition the scenario to make it appear as though someone else is to blame and not take responsibility for your own mistakes.

Dad always says, "When you fall, or make a mistake, pick yourself up and brush yourself off, but never lower your standards." Admitting our mistakes allows us to be vulnerable and vulnerability allows transparency which in turn builds trust.

TOM KROUSE
**President and CEO,
Donatos Pizza–*Respect
the pizza***

*"When I came in as head of marketing, the
advertising at the time reflected the spirit of
Donatos, but it was a little old-fashioned and
entirely focused on selling the benefits of our
product and price point. I just couldn't wait to put
my spin on things, especially to shift away from
functionality and toward entertainment.*

*McDonald's was all for it so we hired a new agency
in the fall of 2000 and were gearing up to run
an ad during the Super Bowl. Our tag line for the
ad–'Respect the pizza'–was meant to send the
message that we were different. For the first
time, we were going with an entertainment ad,
with no call to action and no mention of price
point. We did just one commercial for the Super
Bowl, which featured a guy climbing a mountain
with angels shining a spotlight down on a
Donatos pizza.*

Let's just say our customers didn't know what to make of this approach. The whole campaign was a flop. Lucky for me it didn't hurt sales, but it also didn't make a lick of difference. Not exactly what you hope for when you spend a lot of money on a Super Bowl ad.

I decided I needed to get in front of the whole company, including all of the franchise partners, to apologize for screwing up. Donatos has a forgiving culture, whether it's for a big, expensive mistake or a tiny misstep. The company has turned this attribute into a very powerful tool for self-correcting and making the ongoing adjustments necessary to move forward.

I have made more than my fair share of mistakes. Awareness, forgiveness and acceptance are critical attributes in order to be fully transparent. We must be aware of who we are and accept what we are. You can, however, be transparent without being authentic and lead people to a false perception of who you are. This will destroy trust with people."

HONESTY

Being authentic and transparent begins with being really honest with yourself. It is surprising how long it takes in life to understand what being honest with yourself really means.

Over the years I was surprised by how many gray areas there are in making decisions in business. I remember my dad talking about his experiences and how one of his managers put the cash in his own pocket at the end of the night, or how when he went into business the people around him would tell him not to record all of his sales because he would have to pay taxes. My dad believed that doing things the right way meant being honest in his personal life and in business.

Life is made up of decisions that determine what we are made of and define who we are. The people we choose to surround ourselves with also define who we are. I have learned how important it is to surround yourself as a leader in business and in your home life with positive and honest people.

GREG SERGIO
Director Business Insights,
Donatos Pizza—*Honesty and integrity*

"I started working for Donatos in 1984, when I was a freshman in college. I got a part-time job in the Accounting Department and really took to the work. My supervisor encouraged me to work full time and go to school at night. Eventually, they offered to pay my way through college. It was a great way to learn accounting with terrific hands-on experience working with great people.

The company had already been around for 20 years by the time I got there, so there were a lot of people around me who had been there for 15 years or more. This made a big impression on me, seeing all these loyal, hardworking people who really believed in the company and in Jim.

From my earliest days with the company, I saw a culture that supported honesty. Early on, my direct boss was fresh out of college himself. He had just passed his CPA exam and really thought he was something! He saw everything

Continued on page 130

Continued from page 129

that happened as a stepping-stone for his own progress, and he left as quickly as he could for the next opportunity. This gave me a chance to get a lot of experience and responsibility really quickly, which was incredible.

I ended up getting the most meaningful instruction and guidance from Eleanor White (we call her Whitie). She was a bookkeeper who taught me a lot about accounting, but even more about how to do good work, and especially about how things work at Donatos. She always emphasized to me how important honesty and integrity is to the company. She's a great example of how people pass the Donatos culture along to each other."

(Note: Whitie started with the family in 1975 working as the bookkeeper and retired at age 85 in 2001.)

I learned the importance of hiring the best people possible. Sometimes the best people aren't the most experienced. The best people are the people who can be honest with themselves and with their work experiences. It is important to put systems in place to identify the core values of people and how they will act in certain and uncertain circumstances.

INTEGRITY

I believe that Integrity is an essential attribute for success and clearly a key component of a strong character. To me, it is about doing the right thing simply because it is the right thing to do. The age old advice of "Doing what you say you are going to do, when you say you are going to do it."

It means admitting when you don't know the answer and not being afraid to ask a question. Integrity comes from who you are when no one is looking. Sometimes it simply means being true to your word. I know many business deals were done in the past over a handshake and, unfortunately, people today have good reason not to trust a handshake.

In 2002, I received a phone call from a gentleman named Al who called to ask me if we would sell one of our locations in Philadelphia so that his son Chip could expand his pizza business. I explained to him that our location was not for sale at the time, and if anything were to ever change I would call him.

By the following year our world changed. What had started as rumor, that McDonald's was going to sell the company, became a reality. After the buyback we had to put together a strategy to dispose of all of our excess property.

My first phone call was to Al to let him know that we might be interested in selling. He had his son Chip meet us at the restaurant. Chip immediately put an offer on the table for two restaurants. We negotiated. Caught up in doing a deal and hopeful he could make a go of the restaurants, I signed the deal on a pizza box.

When we returned from our visit we had received a number of phone calls with offers to buy the locations for a lot more money than Chip and

I agreed to that day on the pizza box. While others advised me that we didn't have a legally binding agreement, we had a handshake agreement. We honored our handshake. Today, Chip and his wife have two very successful restaurants.

HUMILITY

I remember the day clearly. Shortly after we bought back the company my father took me to lunch at Lindey's in German Village, near the south side of Columbus, where he grew up.

My dad and I were celebrating the buyback and my new position. As the valet pulled up with his car and we drove away, I remember my father saying to me, "Now Jane, what we did in buying the company back is a good thing and like you said 'it is our destiny'. I just want to caution you not to let success go to your head. Don't let your ego get in your way."

I was so surprised that my father would say that to me for two reasons. One, he is a very humble and grounded person and, secondly, I was a little offended that he would think that I would ever have to worry about my ego.

He said quietly, "Everyone has an ego. Remember you can go as far as you want to as long as you don't care who gets the credit." Words of wisdom from my father, to which I responded, "Dad, I don't have an ego, you don't have to worry about me". Now anyone that has to say they do not have an ego should probably take a good look in the mirror and so I did.

Humility is an easy word to speak about, but it's hard to maintain. There is something that creeps in over time, when you feel the breeze of success, when you are given more responsibilities, or promoted into a position because someone believes in you. Keeping our egos in check is something that we all have to do. It is not our talents or our success that make up the fabric of our being. It is about living a purposeful life and finding life in your purpose.

During the early 90s when we were starting to grow the business, prior to the arches, I had a valuable lesson in humility. We were going to grow, we started franchising, and my father said to me "either go out and hire the experience to report to you or I will hire the person to run the People Department. At the time I was in my mid-20s and remember thinking that he was wrong and I could grow into the job. He challenged me to surround myself with people smarter than me and to get my ego out of the way.

I started a National search for an experienced Human Resource professional. I was really blessed to be able to bring in Ken Williams, the most humble man I've ever met. Genuine, down-to-earth, he had 26 years of experience with Ponderosa as their Senior Vice President of Human Resources. Ken never had a problem reporting to me. He approached it as though he was going to learn as much from me as I could from him. Ken was the best people person and understood the difference between a People Department and a Human Resource Department.

The thing Ken helped us with the most was in writing policies for people. You don't write policies for the exception, you write them for general guidelines. You don't write a policy for one person who decides to show up late and it becomes this huge policy. That is what turns "human resources" into a police department. He single handedly was one of the most influential people to me in my role as Chief People Officer, but unfortunately was only with us for five years.

When McDonald's acquired Donatos, Ken told me, "That's not why I came here. I'm here because of the family business." He had been through acquisitions when he was with Ponderosa and he knew the difference between a family business and a corporation. He no longer wanted to be part of a corporation.

While we were finishing the due diligence for the acquisition, I was attending my orientation with McDonald's and I was seven months pregnant. Ken left in November to become Chief Administration Officer for the Fellowship of Christian Athletes. I delivered in December, on Christmas Eve. With Ken leaving and with my maternity leave falling at the same time, a smooth transition was difficult. I came back and everything had changed. I didn't have Ken to bring continuity to the process. It made the transition complex and created a number of people on-boarding difficulties.

But I learned from the experience. When my dad said, "Either hire someone or I'll hire them for you," it was a humbling statement. The fact that I hired someone who was smarter and had more experience took me outside of my comfort zone but added value to what I was doing. It's a great investment if you have the courage to do it and are serious about learning.

COURAGE

> *"Courage is rightly esteemed the first of human qualities because it is the quality which guarantees all others."*
> **–Winston Churchill**

As stated earlier, to me character is the center of our being, our core, our innermost thoughts and our actions when no one is looking, when we are alone with ourselves, truly alone and it is quiet and all you hear is your heart beating. Your mind is thinking, and you ask the question "who am I"?

Strength of character is critical for successful leaders. But having character without courage limits one's ability to make changes in their company or in the world around them. If we don't have the courage to speak up in a difficult situation, take risks outside of our comfort zone, or bring our principles to work with us, then we begin living in hypocrisy.

Sometimes we believe something so strongly in our heart, but our actions are not aligned because our head convinces us to act within the boundaries of our environment. When our head and heart are not aligned we are in direct conflict with our core value system and start a slow process of a self-fulfilling prophecy of destruction.

Let me give you an early example of Dad's courage. After operating his first store for a few years, my dad decided to expand and opened up two additional restaurants. A few weeks after opening, he would get phone calls late at night from customers telling him that the store ran out of pepperoni and they used salami instead, or they ran out of provolone cheese so they put Parmesan cheese on the pizza.

I remember being a young child and my father making the decision to close the other two restaurants and go back to his first store. This decision was in alignment with his core values. He had the courage to close the restaurants and vowed not to open another restaurant until he was confident that all the processes and systems were in place to ensure consistency at every location.

My dad decided to close the two new stores because he didn't want to disappoint his customers. It took a lot of courage to acknowledge that he wasn't ready to expand until he was 100 percent sure he could provide the same quality product and service every time someone walked through the door of one of his restaurants. Even though closing those stores may have suggested to some people that he had failed, his core belief in providing an excellent, consistent experience was bigger than his fear of failure.

It's in that quiet moment of truth–when you choose to remain aligned with your beliefs in spite of undesirable repercussions–that you get a good look at what you're made of. Those moments usually involve decisions to face up to something small but important, which makes it all the more important to notice those moments, to take care to have the little conversations with yourself that keep you in alignment with your values.

FEAR

People say courage isn't the lack of fear, but the ability to move forward despite your fears. For me, when I think of my experience with courage it is linked closely with my feelings of fear. It may have taken facing my fears to truly appreciate the role courage would play in my leadership. Working in fear is where my "self-fulfilling" spiral began.

It was 9/11/2001 and the whole world, and everybody in it, just seemed to pause. I remember the minute it happened, where I was, with whom I was talking, even what I was wearing. My immediate thoughts went to my three kids. They were at school. My main concern was about their safety. What were they being told?

As I was reassured my children were safe, I immediately went into action to comfort our Donatos family. As a family we had friends and family members who lived in New York. I remember feeling the air was stale. The moments, days and months that followed put a lot of things in perspective and helped people prioritize. We were all feeling a lot of emotions.

Shortly after the world around us changed that September morning we were informed that we needed to "hit our quarterly results to send a message to Wall Street." As I mentioned earlier, this may be the first time ever in my life I actually was told to change the way we operate to hit a quarterly number. We were always focused on beating last year, beating last week, but we never made decisions in order to hit a quarterly budget. Our decisions were about achieving long-term results.

The message came back that we had to do something drastically different by the end of the quarter. We had meeting after meeting to figure out a strategy to make a significant impact so the "Street" would recognize that we were making a change.

We got the message loud and clear that we needed to change our strategy for growth by the end of the quarter. Even though Donatos was hardly on its radar, the "Street" was starting to worry that McDonald's was losing its focus on the core brand.

I understood what would be required to make such a significant change and a number of stores would have to be closed. It wasn't just a store here or there, though; it was going to be the closing of the entire Atlanta market. The decision to close the entire market wasn't logical at the time. Over 50 percent of these restaurants were making money. I had been involved in a family business my whole life, where things were hashed out deliberately and with long-term objectives in mind. This was in conflict with my family business experience.

This is not to disparage public companies in general or McDonald's in particular, but the philosophical difference between how this was playing out on an operational level was different from what I have been taught in a family business. Atlanta was actually a really good market for Donatos. We opened 21 stores in 19 months and they were doing very well. They opened above the national average, and over half of these restaurants were averaging a million dollars in sales. And suddenly we have to close this important market to send a message to Wall Street?

For the first time I started working in fear. What I thought or believed began taking a back seat to my role in this organization. I became very conscious of my role and suddenly found myself with a personal agenda that had never existed before. It was an agenda I was compelled to promote or defend on a daily basis.

Working in fear, my title became more important than my role. I started to care more about who was walking into the boss' office and my own personal agenda than about the culture. It was an awful experience, and at the same time it was a good one for me to have because I had talked about fear all the time, but I had never lived in an environment of fear.

I honestly never knew what working in fear was like. I was not fearful of losing my job. I was not afraid of my financial stability. I was afraid of losing our culture. But going about it, I lost myself in the process.

When you run your own business, it's easier to do right by your principles because all of the decisions–including the hard ones–are your decisions to make. When you work for someone else, finding a way to live your values can be a little trickier, because you're not in the driver's seat. While I didn't personally agree with what was about to happen to those Atlanta stores I wasn't in a position to change the outcome.

I was frustrated by how the process just seemed to be rolling forward. I suddenly realized I had to have the courage to speak up and work with the team to ensure that Our Mission and Promise to our Associates and Customers would be at the core of our decision making process.

CONFLICTED

I was conflicted. I didn't agree with the decision and, despite my emotional attempt to influence the outcomes, I wasn't going to change the decision. Since I couldn't change it, we needed the courage to put a plan together with the

confidence that it was based on Our Mission and
Our Promise.

**Our Mission: To promote goodwill through our
product and service, principles and people.**

**Our Promise: To serve the best pizza and
make your day a little better.**

I remember the day I stopped living in fear. It was
3:00 a.m. and I was at my office trying to figure
out a plan. While I was alone with my thoughts
I was finally able to look at myself in the mirror.
Living in fear created isolation. I couldn't make
decisions. I was paralyzed, micro-managing,
working harder, but with less clarity.

And then in the quiet of the night I realized my
own lights were dimming. I remember reading
a poem my dad had given me in high school,
Desiderata. I walked out of the office that early
morning with a new perspective, with a new
clarity and passion for making a decision based on
the "gray." My light came back.

DESIDERATA

Go placidly amid the noise and haste, and remember what peace there may be in silence.

As far as possible, without surrender be on good terms with all persons. Speak your truth quietly and clearly; and listen to others, even the dull and ignorant; they too have their story. Avoid loud and aggressive persons, they are vexations to the spirit.

If you compare yourself with others, you may become vain and bitter, for always there will be greater and lesser persons than yourself. Enjoy your achievements as well as your plans. Keep interested in your career, however humble; it is a real possession in the changing fortunes of time.

Exercise caution in your business affairs; for the world is full of trickery. But let this not blind you to what virtue there is; many persons strive for high ideals; and everywhere life is full of heroism. Be yourself. Especially, do not feign affection. Neither be critical about love; for in the face of all aridity and disenchantment it is as perennial as the grass.

Take kindly the counsel of the years, gracefully surrendering the things of youth. Nurture strength of spirit to shield you in sudden misfortune. But do not distress yourself with imaginings. Many fears are born of fatigue and loneliness.

Beyond a wholesome discipline, be gentle with yourself. You are a child of the universe, no less than the trees and the stars; you have a right to be here. And whether or not it is clear to you, no doubt the universe is unfolding as it should.

Therefore be at peace with God, whatever you conceive Him to be, and whatever your labors and aspirations, in the noisy confusion of life keep peace with your soul.

With all its sham, drudgery and broken dreams, it is still a beautiful world.

Be cheerful. Strive to be happy.

–Max Ehrmann c. 1920

I was frustrated. While I tried to be respectful in the conversations, I stood up in the middle of a meeting and pounded my fist on the table and said, "If we're going to close this market, we're going to do it the right way. We will not be 'that company' that posts a notice on the door and employees show up for work and find out they don't have a job. We need to make a plan for doing this in a way that promotes goodwill."

The team brought together a plan for how we would close the market with dignity. Dad always taught us to think about what you want to see at the end of any decision. We needed to determine what our end state was going to look like. Our vision, what we wanted to see from this outcome, was to be written up in the Atlanta Business Journal for doing it the right way. We wanted all of our managers to have a job by the end of the two weeks. We wanted to notify our people ahead of time and give them time to discern and plan their future.

If we're going to close a market, which we've never done before, how do you do it, and how do you do it with goodwill? Part of that plan became, first of all, that you communicate the decision and explain the rationale, to people that are impacted ahead of time. A lot of restaurant companies won't tell their people ahead of time because they're worried that people are going to "walk," or afraid they're going to sabotage their brand. They're so afraid of what a few people will do that they don't do the right thing for the whole.

We trust our people every day to serve our customers the product, to take in cash and put it in the register, so why wouldn't we trust them enough to tell them we're going to be closing the doors, and explain what it means to them and how it is going to impact them personally.

We held a job fair at a hotel, where we hosted Boston Market, McDonald's, Wendy's, Burger King– and a number of other local restaurant companies. We coached our managers on how to interview, gave everyone personal and professional references, and introduced them to the companies we hoped would be their future employers. We were proud of the restaurants that stepped up to hire our managers. Some of our franchise partners in neighboring states hired and transferred some of our managers.

This is what we meant by goodwill. We weren't going to close our doors and leave our people with no options. Instead, our managers had jobs within two weeks and all our hourly associates received severance packages. When a decision is difficult to implement, we always fall back on our mission and promise and make sure our actions are in alignment with the decision.

There were our customers to think of as well. Closing a store, defacing the building, is always difficult because of the message it sends to the community. We sent letters to our customers and stayed in the restaurant to talk to customers who called or came in for their last order. It was important that we left the community in the same manner that we entered the community, promoting goodwill.

While the decision to close the market didn't make sense to me, it didn't mean we weren't going to do it and do it the right way. If you must do something, have the courage to do it the right way, do it with integrity, do it with your principles, and do it with grace. In the end, our vision of being written up in the Atlanta Journal Constitution was fulfilled. The Atlanta Journal Constitution wrote an article on the front page of the business section about how we closed the market with goodwill and we did it the right way.

[The Atlanta Journal-Constitution: 11/21/02]

Donatos closes Atlanta eateries, tries to help workers find jobs

By TINAH SAUNDERS
Atlanta Journal-Constitution Staff Writer

Ohio-based Donatos Pizzeria Corp. launched a week of job fairs to place hundreds of displaced employees Wednesday—a day after closing its 23 local restaurants.

Tom Krouse, Donatos' senior vice president of marketing, said the Atlanta area restaurants were closed because sales did not meet expectations.

The chain is owned by McDonald's Corp., which also owns Boston Market.

Donatos, founded in 1963 as a takeout and delivery pizza company, is among the top 15 U.S. pizza chains and has 197 restaurants across the nation. It was recently named Pizza Industry Enterprise of the Year by Pizza Marketing Quarterly, a trade magazine.

The chain entered metro Atlanta in 1998 with four stores in Gwinnett County and expanded rapidly to 23 outlets in mostly suburban locations.

Continued on page 152

Continued from page 151

Donatos' 60 salaried local employees are being offered jobs in either McDonald's or Boston Market restaurants or transfers to other Donatos stores in other states. The company is also offering them outplacement service and counseling as well as a severance package.

The several hundred hourly employees also will receive a week's severance pay, Krouse said.

Although recorded messages on store answering machines say the company hopes to be back in the Atlanta market, Krouse said there are no plans to reopen any of the stores.

"We are reallocating our resources to where we are having the greatest success," Krouse said.

The company had $160 million in sales last year, a 23 percent increase. It also increased the number of its outlets by 26 percent, according to PMQ. It was ranked as the ninth-fastest-growing chain in the United States, based on the increase in sales.

The restaurants, which had colorful but austere interiors and limited table service, did not serve beer or wine. They struggled to compete in the Atlanta market, but Krouse said not selling alcoholic beverages was not a factor.

"We do serve beer in some of our other markets, but that is not a big part of our sales," he said. Atlanta was a learning experience for entering new markets, according to Krouse.

We opened a new store in Munich, Germany, last week–our first international location–with full table service.

I learned a lot about fear and courage during that period, but I also discovered that it takes courage to do a lot of "every day ordinary" things. For example, it takes courage to make mistakes. Many of us move through life carefully avoiding errors. We stay in our lanes, color inside the lines, don't speak until spoken to–all to eliminate the chance we might make a mistake that imperils our safety and security. And yet for every mistake we manage to avoid, we also miss the chance to learn from it and to stretch and grow.

> *"Anyone who has never made a mistake has never tried anything new.*
> *"Learn from yesterday, live for today, hope for tomorrow. The important thing is to never stop questioning."*
> **–Thomas Edison**

I learned that it also takes courage to be curious. Curiosity is hard-wired to take you out of your comfort zone. In fact, it can take you so far out of your comfort zone it can be downright dangerous! And yet some of the most amazing things in your work and personal life wouldn't happen if you didn't have the courage to be curious. Innovation doesn't happen without curiosity behind it.

CONVICTION

I have found along my journey that many people find themselves in a job because it provides an income and financial stability. I believe that successful people are different. They have found their true purpose in life.

What is my purpose? Why am I here? How can I make a difference? Is the life I'm living worth the price I am paying? The questions came from my reading of the *Purpose Driven Life,* by Rick Warren. But I also learned it takes courage to ask yourself these big questions because the answers–or the lack of answers–can reveal just how far you are from your purpose.

The biggest clue that you have veered from your purpose–or have been operating without a purpose entirely–is that vague, nagging feeling that you're not happy in your work, or life. You can go a long time ignoring that feeling because of concerns about income and financial security. But it's not going to go away, no matter how many promotions or raises you receive. And conviction is one thing that can help you do something about it. To me conviction is the act of living out your purpose with passion.

When one is committed to their purpose there is a true satisfaction in what they do for a living. They no longer look at life as making a living but are living a life with purpose. It takes conviction to find your purpose in life and passion to express it in what you do for a living.

Is the life you are living worth the price you are paying? Sometimes people settle for things because they get caught up in life. We settle for a "job" because we have to provide for our families and we lose sight of our dreams.

Many people have passion and stand for something but few people are passionate about their purpose. It is critical to have passion with a purpose. So we ask ourselves what is our purpose? Why are we here? How can we make a difference?

My entire family has demonstrated the courage to follow their passion in many different entrepreneurial ways, which are all different than following the family business. In addition, my son, Tony Capuano, decided after he graduated from college that he wanted to create a space where people could grow mentally, spiritually, physically and emotionally. He invested in and is now operating five SNAP Fitness centers.

KAREN KUNTZ

Franchise Business Consultant, Donatos Pizza—*I know what my job is—to follow the promise*

"I have been at Donatos for 23 years. Before coming here, I was with a national pizza company for 15 years that saw Donatos as their biggest threat in the markets where they both compete. In comparing the two, the national company's focus was on the numbers (financial) and the process. At Donatos the focus is on people and product.

When I first started at Donatos I was a manager in training. Despite the fact that I had managed stores before, I had to learn the Donatos way. Why did I change? Before I never felt valued. My opinions didn't matter. What I love about Donatos is I know every day what my job is—to follow the promise—make someone's life a little better.

I love to solve problems. I find my energy in the stores. I have always said it's about building an environment where I want my daughter to work, to learn responsibility, to show up on time, and be held accountable for high expectations. It was great when my daughter wrote her school paper about me—my passion for my job.

I remember when I was working in our stores there was a young associate who was having problems with her family. Her mother was addicted to drugs and it embarrassed the daughter. I told her it was about her, being herself, finding her own purpose in life. There was nothing she couldn't do, if she put her mind to it. Today's she is a prominent attorney in our town. It's another way we can make someone's life better.

Now, in our franchise operations, I am part of what we call our 'Promise Team.' We are taking Donatos to new markets, communicating what our product is, developing people to fulfill our promise, and by making their life a little better, they will treat our customers better. We do it by setting the example and in the long term by having fun.

People say that young people today are different. The biggest difference I see is that it's harder to train them to look at the customer. They are used to looking at their phones. But, when you set the example, make it fun and tell them why, they are willing to work hard to earn our 'High Five' and 'Top Ten' pins. They like the recognition."

PERSEVERANCE

I had periods of time when I wasn't sure that I loved what I was doing. This caused internal conflict because it was a family business. I loved our mission, our people and our product, but I didn't love what I was doing anymore.

Reflecting on my difficult times I realized that I either didn't like who I was working for, or I didn't like the person I was becoming. It is easy to find reasons not to "like" the person you are working for; it is much harder to look in the mirror and recognize that you might not like the person you are becoming.

When we look for the negative in others we can find it. However, when we try to sense our own opportunities our vision becomes blurred. When we love what we do, but don't like the people we are working for, it causes us to question our journey.

If we have conviction for what we are doing there is nothing that will stop us from achieving great results. We learn that everyone has something to teach us and we are open to learning from everyone.

I became stronger in my conviction when the path was the hardest. Something about obstacles, whether they are real or perceived, creates determination and perseverance. The tough times allow us to build perseverance, which in turn builds character.

We can also lose our sense of purpose when we are put into situations that cause us to compromise. When we compromise on who we are and what we stand for it is easy to blame others and become a victim.

If we have conviction, we will not compromise. If we love what we are doing, we will persevere. Our behavior will reflect our values. When we compromise we lose a little self worth and begin to accept mediocrity.

Conviction comes from an attitude of continuous learning, self-awareness and faith. When you know you are fulfilling your heart's desire and you have the courage to remove obstacles you can achieve anything. Believing in something greater than yourself creates new paths of learning.

Removing your ego and recognizing that what you are isn't nearly as important as who you are is an important step in achieving your purpose. Being curious is courageous. Being courageous is contagious. When you have conviction you allow yourself to take risks you wouldn't normally take in business and in your personal life.

THE RIGHT REASON

In February 2003, a rumor began circulating that McDonald's was going to sell Donatos. McDonald's was shifting away from its "meal occasion" strategy, which included a brand portfolio of hamburger, chicken, Mexican and pizza, back to its core brand.

I remember the day as clearly as if it was yesterday. My father came into my office and sat down. Before he could even get a word in edge wise, I said "Dad, let's buy the company back from McDonald's," I was enthusiastic and excited with the thought of owning the company again. I said "We have 5,000 people who are committed to our mission and promise. We have a destiny." I told him I had the passion and energy and would do whatever it took to get our company back. I said, "I will put everything I have back into this company. I just know we have a future that is far greater than where we are today. I believe this is our destiny."

I told him I needed his leadership and vision to pull this off. And frankly, I also needed his money!

Here is a man who spent his entire life building and running two companies, and now that he was in a position to enjoy the fruits of all that hard work, I was asking him to get back in business with me. And he didn't hesitate for a minute. "Are you up to the task?" was all he asked. I was not only up for it, I was already charging ahead on it, quickly putting together a team of experts to help us do it.

One of the best things that happened to our family was McDonald's buying the company. This allowed the family to pursue their passions and purposes in life without the emotional connection of staying with the family business. I had to make sure that my passion for buying the company back was for the right reasons.

People often ask me why I would risk everything I had gained from the sale of our company to McDonald's to buy it back when the company was losing money and I could easily have walked away and let things fold. All I can say in response is that I had never been more certain of my purpose in my whole life, and that I just knew that Donatos had a destiny that had yet to be fulfilled.

I never stopped and even questioned whether we should pursue the re-purchase. I believed that we had the best people and that their passion would turn the company around. I knew the decision was the right decision, but I had to ask myself a question. In my quest and passion to purchase the company back, was I doing it for the right reason?

Was I so determined to get the company back because we had so many great people who believed in our mission and promise, or was I trying to make my dad proud? As vulnerable as that statement is to write, I have found so many people in a family business stay in the business for different reasons.

Many second and third generation family members have an emotional connection and find it difficult to separate from the family ties. Sometimes the family stays in the business to make their parents proud. While others stay in the business because they have not had the opportunity to work anywhere else and feel a sense of safety and security.

No matter which angle I considered, the answer was very clear. This was the moment in my professional life when my passion and purpose was right there in front of me–we were not just buying back a company, we were investing in our people, our family and our future.

INFLUENCE THE OUTCOME

Once we made the decision to buy the company back, we went to work on creating a strategy. Tom Krouse, who was then our Chief Marketing Officer, and I put together a plan and designed an organization to support three different scenarios.

We went off-site and worked on one plan where we bought the whole company back and grew the company, one where we minimized our risk and closed the outside markets, and one where we franchised the outside markets and kept our core market as a company. Each strategy had significantly different scenarios in regard to our structure.

One day, late in October 2003, we stood in front of McDonald's Brand Board of Advisors. Our then CFO presented his sell/close plan (Plan A), while I presented our team's plan to buy back the company (Plan B).

On December 11, 2003 my father and I signed the papers to buy the company from McDonald's. We believe in the power of ownership and held a percentage for each member of the executive team to purchase a share at the same price we paid. My mom, brothers and sister all reinvested because they believed in the destiny of Donatos' people.

As I wrote a check for my share of the purchase, it may have been the first time I recognized the difference between thinking like an owner and signing the *front* of the check versus the *back* of the check. Granted, I have been an owner most of my life, due to great estate planning by my parents. However, this was different; I signed the front of the check and became a partner with my dad. And I never looked back, never questioned my decision, and never thought for one second that we weren't pointed in just the right direction we should be going.

The leadership at McDonald's was very supportive and we had met with them over several months to propose a few ideas. They believed in our mission and wanted to see the family buy the company back. They wanted to see us succeed. We were fortunate to be working with people of integrity.

However, we were still buying back an unprofitable company with a lot of debt. The first year we had a $10.5 million turn around which I attribute to our people and our store managers. They continued to be the face of the company to our customers. Another "turn around" was attributed to our customers' perceptions.

After the buyback, there were many people that told us our pizza again tasted like it did before the McDonald's purchase. The truth is that throughout the time we were "under the arches" we never changed the recipe, or any of the quality ingredients. Yet the perception was that the taste had changed. It confirmed what my dad has always said, "Pizza made with love nourishes your soul." Apparently the way our pizza is made (with love) and delivered by our people (with a smile) made the difference.

> *"The palate is the last thing you use for taste."*
> **–Mark Reed, Executive Director**
> **Purchasing & Supply Chain,**
> **Donatos Pizza**

All of our people continued to fulfill our mission and promise, and never wavered from their passion for our customers, our product and our people. It was our people that had the conviction. Our people stood strong and believed in the destiny of Donatos–they are the reason for the turn around.

My father focused on the finances and the commitments made during the "years under the arches". Doug Kourie, our current CFO, was one of our first hires. It was so important for us to bring on a CFO that understood both the dynamics of a family business and the workings of a large public company. Doug had worked as our auditor previously and was perfect for the job. Not only did he have restaurant experience at a public company, but more importantly for us, he knew how to work with a family-owned business in a turnaround situation.

DOUG KOURIE
Chief Financial Officer, Donatos Pizza–
Goodwill is an accounting term

"I knew that the technical part of the job would be difficult, cleaning up some of the things McDonald's had done. I also knew, however, that Donatos really lives their mission of goodwill. I saw it first hand when I was their auditor years before. Now I remind our associates from time to time that goodwill is also an accounting term. Your value to the community is worth more than the sum of your assets."

Tom Krouse, in a new role of Chief Concept & Strategy Officer, led our growth strategy. He worked with the team to build the right size asset and a new concept for the future. I spent the next three years visiting our stores learning what we were doing right and what we were doing wrong.

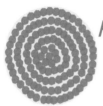

ANNIE UPPER

**(Formerly Nancy Grote), Founding
Family Member and Jane's Mother—**
Empathy and compassion

*"For me, empathy and compassion come from being
a woman and a mother. I just took those natural
inclinations with me into my work at Donatos. I
think that people make lots of mistakes in life, but
every time they make a mistake, they have a chance
to do things differently. It's what you do after you
make a mistake that determines your path.*

*I have a great belief in people, so I felt it was
important for our people to understand that
Donatos was an environment where they could
make a change in their lives–to grow or just to
have a better experience. This compassionate
environment was very purposefully cultivated,
starting at the very beginning with Jim and carried
into the present day by Jane.*

*I believe that many of our best managers and
associates were able to realize their potential
because they learned they had the authority
to make their own decisions."*

We rolled out a new restaurant concept, started Jane's Dough Bakery, improved our income statement and began to franchise once again. I never looked back and I believe that our stores make a difference in the lives of the associates and the customers that they serve every day.

COMPASSION

If you were to take a personality profile and one of your core strengths happens to be compassion, the career choices presented to you are often reserved for medicine, nurses, doctors, non-profit organizations and even the teaching profession. It is rare to have a personality profile encourage a career as a business CEO, lawyer or entrepreneur if your core strength is compassion.

The trait of compassion seems to be reserved for people who are going through a difficult situation, bereavement or some degree of crisis. It takes a certain type of person to have the nurturing ability of a nurse or a doctor. But I don't think we should underestimate the need for compassion in leadership. Compassion is the ability to act in fairness, with love and kindness. Why wouldn't we hold our leaders to these traits in business?

While compassion is an easy principle, or character trait, to talk about, it can be difficult to follow in all situations. I must admit that when one of our managers faces the threat of a burglary, or a driver a robbery, or we have to let someone go because they mistreated an associate, or a customer, or stole money, it can be difficult to have compassion.

When people make decisions that are contradictory, or destructive, it is difficult to express compassion. People misinterpret compassion for acceptance of behavior. It doesn't mean that the behavior is acceptable, or that people are not held accountable. It is having compassionate accountability and we do it through what our now CEO Tom Krouse developed–Donatos Success Behaviors reflecting the "balance" between what we call the head and the heart.

The behaviors are listed in two general categories. The first is opportunity-seeking, symbolized by the passion we feel in our heart. This is the entrepreneurial spirit that drives us to find opportunities, create excitement, build enthusiasm, act like an owner and accomplish tasks.

The second is discipline, symbolized by the focused clarity we have in our mind. This is the logical, strategic, fact based approach to doing business that focuses all our passionate enthusiasm toward the activities that will make a difference.

The key is to maximize both categories of behaviors. All passion with no discipline is tireless, direction-less energy. Likewise, all logical strategy with no motivation, leadership or action is purely an intellectual exercise. When we plan our actions and execute with boundless excitement, we will always create success for the entire family.

FIRST SEEK TO UNDERSTAND

Since we all have different experiences in life and come from different paradigms, many people do not know how others would want to be treated in certain circumstances. It is a difficult task to fully understand how the other person would want to be treated when you haven't walked in their shoes.

I learned early on about compassion from my mother and father. My father was consistent with practicing his principles with every decision he made in the business. When my mother joined the business she brought along her compassion. She truly embodied the ability to better understand what a person may have been going through in their life experiences.

My mother worked in both Human Resources and Real Estate, two professions that are not typically under one leader. But my mom had the unique ability to pick the best locations (real estate) and the best people (HR). She relied on both her intelligence and intuition. She created the expectation that we must first seek to understand then to be understood. We apply this principle in everything we do, especially when there are barriers for people to perform at high levels in the Donatos family.

LOVE YOUR WAY THROUGH IT

My best piece of advice in life, personally and professionally, was from my father–to "love your way through it". He said this to me over and over again. I learned that it is easy to love your way through life when there are no obstacles. However, when challenges arise and you are met with resistance, it requires compassion to love your way through the circumstances.

This doesn't mean taking the easy way out or to simply avoid talking about the difficulties in life and business. It means being honest, but with kindness. It means facing your fears with forgiveness and stretching yourself to take risks.

Talking about love in business is not a common core value that is expressed in describing how people must act in their daily lives. But it is important to recognize that if we aspire to love in life, in our work, and in our homes we must demonstrate the ability to show compassion.

THE GOLDEN RULE

My father was taught a valuable lesson at the early age of 13, regarding the importance of treating others the way you want to be treated. Although he grew up in a principle centered home where treating others the way you want to be treated was common practice, he learned that this simple principle wasn't always practiced in business.

Whether he was told to water down the sauce to get more pizzas by the end of the shift, or not to show all his sales so he wouldn't have to pay taxes, he realized that these directions were in contradiction with his core values. He wanted to create a place where people could bring their principles to work with them.

My father never wavered in his principles whether it was a business acquisition, real estate negotiation, customer transaction or associate interaction. My father believed that every encounter should be one where people are treated as he would want to be treated. This might sound like a simple principle but, unfortunately, there are times in business where it becomes secondary.

Over the years we have incorporated the principle of 'treating others the way you want to be treated' in our training for hourly associates and home office staff. It has become our golden rule for decision-making. I believe that truly understanding this principle requires one to fully understand and respect how people want to be treated in the first place.

SOFT OR TOUGH?

We must have compassion for people and better understand their personal experiences. Compassion in business may often be looked upon as a weak or soft way of doing business.

I believe that having compassion is the strongest character trait a leader can have in any business. While compassion isn't all encompassing, I do believe that one must truly love, be kind, honest and warm hearted when dealing with people and making decisions.

Many people jump to the conclusion that you have to be tough in business and that there is no room for a "soft approach" to business decisions. But, it is much easier to avoid difficult discussions than it is to allow the human value of love to enter the equation. Loving one another is a simple human value.

It has always been interesting to me that people view the most important part of their business—people—as the "soft stuff". People are the business. People, in both good times and hard times, make up our culture and are the expression of what we stand for. I believe the most compassionate people are also the toughest.

INVEST IN ENGAGED PEOPLE

When we talk about a balance sheet and the numbers on the profit and loss statement we can be objective, make decisions and build our strategy. Executing the strategy without the ability to comprehend how it affects people leaves businesses with hollow mission statements and people who are not engaged. The old saying that people don't care how much you know until they

know how much you care is a true statement.
Once we realize that the strategy cannot be
executed without people who are fully engaged
we have to ask ourselves the question, "Why
wouldn't we invest in our people as our greatest
asset?" But understanding that people are
human and make mistakes requires an honest
environment of trust and respect.

I believe Jack Welch in his book *Straight from the
Gut* said it best when he stated, "The kindest
thing you can do for someone is to be honest
with them". But I think this statement is missing
one key ingredient. The kindest thing you can
do for someone is to be honest with them—with
compassion.

Pure honesty without compassion can be brutal.
Being honest with your associates and with
your business partners is a critical component
to success. Honesty builds trust and trust builds
rela1tionships. We are in a relationship era and
there are few businesses that do not count on
relationships to build their business, whether it is
a relationship with your customer, your associate
and/or your business partner. ♥

THE MISSING PIECE Jane Grote Abell

CHAPTER 3
PEOPLE

Even before the role of Chief People Officer existed at Donatos, it was my passion. I learned from a very young age how important our people were to the success of our company, or any organization. It was part of my dad's dream–*creating an environment where people could learn about honesty, integrity and coming to work on time.*

Working side by side with our people in our restaurants since I was a teenager, I could see that we all shared a sense of pride in our product and cared deeply about the company's relationship with the community. From my ground-level experience in the organization, I had a pretty clear idea of what it took for an associate to do well and the critical role that a manager plays in a store's success.

When I graduated from The Ohio State University in 1988 with a degree in Organizational Design and Communication, I honestly wasn't sure what direction in the company I wanted to pursue but I knew I had a natural affinity for our people. I took a position as a training manager in our Training Department, reporting to Charlene Rose-Stetler, Tim Young and Curtis Elder who had been with Donatos for more than 30 years in various positions. I loved that job and really enjoyed working closely with the managers of restaurants.

In the Training Department I was under the direction of my mom who was responsible for the Real Estate and People Departments. She has a passion for helping people learn and grow. Mom was one of the founding mothers of Amethyst, a non-profit organization whose mission is to foster a culture of recovery, empowering women and families in a safe, sober community.

Two years later in 1990, the position of Personnel Manager became available. My older brother Tom who was our Chief Operations Officer at the time, encouraged me to interview for the job. Tom has always been my biggest fan and the one to encourage me to learn more, do more and take more risks. He always believed in me, even when I didn't have confidence in myself.

With my degree and my work experience in
the restaurants, I knew enough about how an
organization should run and how communication
within a company should happen, but didn't feel
I had the skill set or practical knowledge to get in
the "people business" within our company. And yet
I had a good idea that this is where I wanted to go,
so I asked to interview for this position. I was one
of several candidates for the job and I admit that I
was at a distinct disadvantage due to my personal
circumstances.

I was a single parent at the time and working in the
restaurants was proving to be increasingly difficult.
My son Tony was two years old, and everyone in
the family worked in the business, so there was
little availability for family childcare support during
the week. I worked a lot of nights, so my younger
sister Katie offered to babysit on the weekends, and
I'd pick him up at her house at 2:00 in the morning.
But this was tough on my son, my sister and me.

Katie grew up and worked in the stores like I did.
She managed our Catering Department working
with Charlene Rose. Katie brought a people
perspective to catering. She created a system

for serving customers with large orders. Katie is an artist and brings a creative mind and an empathetic heart to every aspect of her life. She helped me learn how to bring my heart into business decisions.

I was learning the hard way how critical good, dependable child care was for a single working mom. I knew I would have to find a way to work out my child-care issue if I wanted to be given serious consideration for this new position. I called Action for Children, a local nonprofit that provides childcare and parent support services. The program ended up making a world of difference for my son, giving him safe, consistent care and a high-quality early childhood development experience.

For me, it provided just the kind of child-care partnership I needed to be able to take the next step within our company. I interviewed with my mom for the position. Up against experienced and knowledgeable candidates I still remember the day clearly. And I remember how serious I felt the potential opportunity was. I became Personnel Manager in 1990, beginning an incredible period of growth and learning in my own career.

Two things were working in my favor: First, my mom and dad believed in me and gave me a lot of room to understand and master the job. Secondly, my lack of experience actually made me wide open to learning and taking risks. When we were growing up, my father taught us to ask questions when we didn't understand something, so we learned to solve problems by asking a lot of questions, always trying to understand the "why" behind a decision or situation.

He insisted that we know how to challenge the norm and to defend our own positions as well. Having a curious mind was a priority for my dad. So was the power of positive thinking. He read Napoleon Hill's *Think and Grow Rich* at an early age and it made a tremendous impression on him. Even when we were very young, he taught us to use positive thoughts to craft our destiny and to visualize what we wanted to happen in our lives. My dad and mom have always had a thirst for spiritual and intellectual growth.

PUTTING PEOPLE FIRST

After accepting the position of Personnel Manager, I went to work learning the technical

skills associated with the job. I had never
worked for any company but Donatos, so I had
no preconceived notion of what a Personnel
Department should be. I realized pretty quickly
that there were a lot of rules and regulations,
paperwork, processes and policies that we needed
to put in place. We had long had the heart of
the company in the right place, but a lot of the
structure needed to follow. I also began to see that
the more time I spent working on these policies,
the less time I had to spend with our people.

Almost immediately, I decided to pursue a
Professional in Human Resources Certification.
This would involve time-consuming study for
the four-hour PHR exam, which I thought would
shore me up given my lack of HR experience. My
head quickly filled with enormous amounts of
information about employment laws, payroll taxes,
workers' compensation, pension plans and benefits.
I knew it was important to learn all of this; the
information is valuable to any organization.

But while I was studying, I couldn't help
noticing that the certification wasn't focused on

ensuring one's ability to work with people–how to treat people, how to hire the right people, how to cultivate a positive culture, or how to terminate people in a humane and respectful way. Instead, it was about learning how to avoid making legal or ethical mistakes in the role–in other words, protecting the company not the people.

I was up late studying on the night before the exam when I got a call from Mark Reed, who was Director of Purchasing and Distribution and a long time Donatos associate. "Jane," he said in a somber voice, "the police just called to say they believe that one of our associates was in a fatal accident." He worked for us in our Donatos Food Service warehouse and his step-mom was one of my first mentors outside of my family.

"Where are you?" I asked, my mind racing and my heart sinking. "I'm headed to the morgue to ID the body," he answered. "I'll meet you there," I said, not knowing what the next hours would entail or how much they would change my perspective on my work.

MARK REED
**Executive Director Purchasing
& Supply Chain, Donatos Pizza—**
A member of our family

"When I received the call, the first person I thought to call was Jane. It was a member of our 'family' and I knew I needed to let her know. What do I mean by family? It's a feeling that you don't have to put on a different hat when you come to work than the one you have at home.

That's why I joined the crisis team and also why I knew I had to be back in the office first thing in the morning to share the news with the rest of our family."

I was nervous but calm when I met up with Mark at the morgue, and silently praying that it wasn't our associate. The air was stale and temperature cold in the room where we waited. After a few minutes, attendants wheeled a gurney into an area behind a glass window, where we could see the body covered with a blood stained sheet. The person behind the window pulled the sheet back from the top and Mark and I knew immediately it was one of us, one of the Donatos family. We were stunned, speechless.

All of 24 years old at the time, I didn't have any idea what would come next after we identified the body. So when the police officer asked us if we wanted to go with them to tell the parents, we had to stop and think. As much as we loved his mom and dad, I wanted to be able to be there to hug them when they found out the terrible news. But Mark and I agreed that we needed to put ourselves in their shoes and recognize their need for privacy in that tragic moment.

I vividly remember leaving the morgue that night. The moon was full, the night was dark and I was so sad. By this time, it was after 3:00 in the morning and all I wanted to do was get home and hug my son. But in a few short hours, I had to take that test. After all that preparation, the test hardly mattered to me anymore. Before I got that call from Mark, all I could think of was passing that test to prove myself worthy of my new position.

But driving home that night, I realized that HR didn't have anything to do with what I'd been studying or the initials that would come after my name if I passed that test. It was suddenly very simple and clear to me—Human Resources was about the people. What test could prepare someone for responding to a situation like the one I had just faced? What textbook could teach someone compassion, or empathy, or respect for another person's dignity?

The next morning, I went to take the test, which ironically was being held in the building right next to the morgue where I had been just hours before. I remember sitting in the lobby for a few minutes before going in for the test. All I could think of was our associate laying in the morgue, and the anguish his mom and dad must have been feeling at that very moment. I don't remember a thing about the exam.

That experience brought everything my mother taught me about compassion into focus. She believed that good business decisions require a balance between your head and your heart. The way we treat our people in difficult situations, how we take care in shaping their professional experience, and how we celebrate individual achievement in our Donatos family all make our mission come alive through our people.

Human Resources is so much more than getting annual reviews done, designing a benefits plan, or processing workers' compensation. All of these efforts have an important impact on the business, but ultimately it all comes down to the Golden Rule and my dad's fundamental belief in treating others the way you want to be treated. From a Human Resources perspective, this can mean the difference between a culture of process and a culture of people.

CHANGING AS WE GROW

In the early 90s, my brother Tom led our efforts to grow the family business through franchising. This was an exciting but challenging endeavor. Tom put together a team to ensure we attracted the best people as franchisees; after all, signing a franchise agreement would make the franchisee a part of our family for 20 years!

Tom worked with the team and a consultant to create a profile of the type of franchise partners we wanted to work with and become part of Donatos. An important part of that discussion was about the words we use to describe our people and our business. This conversation led to the creation of the Donatos Dictionary to ensure that we were using certain words purposefully and consistently to convey our values across the organization.

For example, we looked carefully at the word "franchisee," which in our industry represents an individual's investment in a business in the form of licensing fees and a portion of profits. The type of franchise relationships we hoped to build wasn't really reflected in the word "franchisee," so we chose instead to use the term "franchise partner" which more accurately represents what we see as a partnership in our business.

Similarly, we refer to our corporate offices as the "home office" rather than "headquarters" and our employees as "associates," in both cases to reflect our emphasis on our larger Donatos family. We refer to our vendors as "business partners" to make it clear that we're in this together.

FROM THE DONATOS DICTIONARY

Paradigm-Shift Definitions

From	To
$ Per Man Hour	$ Per Person Hour
Acquisition/Compromise	Partnership/Synergy
Corporate Headquarters	Home Office
Dough Room	Bakery
Employees	Associates
Franchisee	Franchise Partner
Human Resources	People Services
Man Planning	People Planning
Manage	Lead
Royalty	Licensing Fee
Train	Teach
Unit	Store/Restaurant
Vendor	Business Partner

MARK REED

**Executive Director Purchasing
& Supply Chain, Donatos Pizza—**
Is that fair?

"There are so many examples of how we view our relationships differently. My first example came within two weeks of my joining Donatos. There was a problem with the colors on our business cards. The printer agreed to reprint the order ($400 to $500).

I went to Jim to let him know, thinking he would be pleased, but instead he asked, 'Is that fair?' He thought paying them $150 for their materials and time would be fair. That's when I started to realize what being a business partner really meant.

Today our business partners have been with us on average between 10 to 12 years. There are many items we single source. When we are 'negotiating' we don't back people into a corner. We look for and find the middle ground. It's a relationship. We treat them as partners and we know if there are problems they will respond."

As we discussed the vocabulary we wanted to use to describe our business relationships, it dawned on us that the term "Human Resources Department" was not an accurate reflection of our particular sensibility about our associates. So we changed the name to the People Department, to make very clear that our people were our priority and that our systems would be designed to support the growth and development of everyone in our Donatos family.

CHIEF PEOPLE OFFICER

I remember talking to my brother and dad about how a people-first environment might be a key ingredient missing in our industry. My brother Tom really inspired me and joined in promoting the idea. The Chief Executive Officer creates the vision for an organization. The CEO then relies on the Chief Financial Officer to oversee the financial health of the company. And a Chief Operating Officer executes the business strategy and produces results.

Businesses that reflect a strong people centered company recognize the unique benefit of having a strong Human Resources presence–a Chief People Officer–at the executive table. (If neither the CEO nor the Human Resources director understands how important this is, you've got a CEO who may be the wrong person for the job and an HR executive who is behaving like a personnel manager.)

How does the Chief People Officer differ from the traditional HR leadership role? First, the Chief People Officer should be a genuine partner with the CEO, with a unique level of trust between the people in these two roles. The Chief People Officer is charged with developing, sustaining or improving the systems that create a culture with a soul. The CPO must chart the journey for every individual in the organization, providing a road map for success for the company that can only be achieved when the individuals succeed.

It is the responsibility of the entire leadership team to carry out the Mission. But it is the role of the Chief People Officer (CPO) to chart the journey by giving the organization a road map for success through people. Attracting, hiring, training, retaining and developing talent is critical to every organization, but where traditional HR tends to institutionalize this function, the CPO understands that these efforts are the result of specific people-focused acts of leadership, not rote policy and process.

The difference between the two approaches can be seen when HR becomes more of a police department. Writing policies for the whole, instead of dealing with the exception, and keeping the whole healthy is how trust is built. But it takes a kind of courage to break away from the comfort and rigor of those policies and processes.

Once you commit to doing the right thing for your people—in how you build systems to advance their growth and development, in how you respond to unexpected events, in how you handle difficult conversations—this approach simply makes more sense than any other. When a company's leadership team truly cares about the people and holds everyone accountable for behaviors in the organization that are not in alignment with the "people principle," the value of all the organization's human assets can be realized.

In my role as Chief People Officer, I discovered that the difference between a people-first approach and a traditional systems-oriented HR approach was especially clear when it came to our response when we made a mistake. Every business makes them, whether it's hiring the wrong person for the job, making a decision without all the facts in front of you, or changing course without communicating well with your organization.

Any one of these mistakes will cut deep into the balance in your trust account. The challenge is in responding to the error in a way that conveys your continued commitment to respecting and caring for your people. When a leader doesn't take appropriate action in response to a mistake, she sends a message to the organization that whatever happened is acceptable. If poor performance is ignored or excused, it sends a message to high performers that their efforts are not appreciated. If bad behavior is allowed, fear will creep into the veins and arteries of the company.

CHERYL BERGSMAN
Director Operations Development, Donatos Pizza–*Letting people make mistakes*

"When I'm working to develop supervisors or managers, I think hands-on experience is the most important. Sometimes this means throwing away the play book and letting people make mistakes under my supervision. I toss them into the deep end of the pool, then work with them to learn how to make confident decisions and solve problems.

Mistakes are made, but being able to make those decisions is very empowering. I get them to learn my job, which can be intimidating, but it's a great way to learn how to make decisions."

The organization has to create a culture where people trust the leadership to acknowledge, understand the impact of, and appropriately respond to a mistake–we call it compassionate accountability. It's one of the most important ways to ensure that your people have full confidence that you will do the right thing by them, starting with your customers, your business partners, and the communities where you do business. It's embedded in our Mission. The best thing you can do to show people how much you care is to create a trusting environment.

My brother Tom built our organization chart like a circle and as a family our job was to "shine the light." We use an illustration to help our Donatos family understand that they have the power and choice to keep the light shining.

The light–Our Mission–has to be carried through all of the layers of the organization. At any given moment, any one person can block the light–the mission to promote goodwill through product and service, principles and people–from shining through to the person next to him, all the way to our customers.

When someone blocks the light–for reasons as simple as having a bad day and taking it out on a colleague or as serious as a manager having an inappropriate interaction with an associate–the organization is empowered to correct it. At any one point, any one person can block the light. When this happens we have to empower everyone to shine the light again. If we don't, we risk losing the trust that is necessary to maintain everyone's personal connection to the mission.

SUCCESSION PLANNING

Not all Human Resource professionals can be Chief People Officers. The difference is in how the leadership team behaves. It isn't in the position, or the title. It is about actions. It is having the courage to do what is right, because it is the right thing to do for the people. It is about the gray areas in business. It is engineering the systems for people development and growth. It is how we handle difficult conversations.

It is about having people in leadership positions that genuinely care about people and holding everyone, starting with the CEO, accountable when behaviors are not in alignment. It means living above the line, being steadfast to the mission.

Providing constant support for our team's growth and development is intrinsic to our culture, and performance reviews are one of the ways we measure progress and potential, and identify the ways we can best invest in our people. One of the tools we use is a simple quadrant rating system that helps determine where people are in relation to our mission, the people in our company that are promotable and the people that might be 'blocking the light.'

On a monthly, quarterly and annual basis, the associates in the home office and managers of the restaurants participate in a development discussion about performance (results) and core principles (behavior). The information derived from these conversations rate people in two categories–principles and results–and places them into one of the following quadrants:

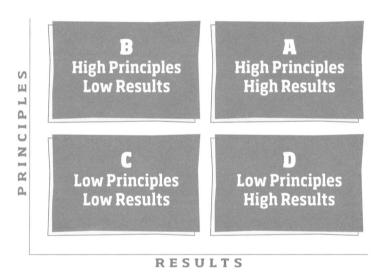

When someone is placed in the A quadrant (High Principles, High Results), he or she is considered very promotable within the company. People placed in the B quadrant are people we will work with on a development plan in order to improve their results. People who are placed in the C quadrant (Low Principles, Low Results) will become Donatos alumni. And finally, those individuals who fall in the D quadrant (Low Principles, High Results) will be asked to become alumni.

This is surprising to some because the "high results" aspect of the D quadrant may normally cause management to sidestep the problem of low core principles or to look the other way. Who can resist someone who produces great results, even if they're toxic to the people around them? Many might say they are the ones who are making money for the organization. You should keep them, maybe help them on their values, hoping they would do no harm. Those in traditional HR may even warn–you have to keep them, there is no basis upon which to terminate, they are getting the results required.

But we disagree. Results without principles can be too high of a price to pay. The lack of values "blocks the light" and can lead to long-term damage to the people (especially those who report to the person) and the organization. It is important to our company's core to help them become alumni when they don't exhibit our core principles. We have found that while results are compelling, seeing the company's mission and principles displayed in a person's work is even more compelling.

It takes a lot of courage for a manager to say, "You've got great numbers, but your behavior doesn't align with our core values." Getting rid of the negativity–the light blockers–is one of the most important tasks you have, as it unleashes the positive potential in everyone else. Once the blocker is removed (compassionate accountability), the light shines even brighter. But when it happens it's important that it be done with dignity and goodwill.

Whether it's a bad company policy or a person's outlook or behavior that blocks the light, it's important that the trust is strong enough in all directions to be able to point out the inconsistency, or flaw, so that everyone in the organization can prosper.

It's also important to create opportunities for people to learn, train and advance in their career, as the personal gratification that comes from that growth is what makes the light bright in the first place. That's what we do with those in quadrant B (High Principles, Low Results).

Their principles are aligned, but they aren't yet achieving the results. We help them by guiding them in how to achieve the result. There are many stories of our associates who believed in and followed our principles and with coaching became very successful.

COMPASSIONATE ACCOUNTABILITY

Another critical aspect to our people-focused approach is to express the compassion that is so important to our mission, at the same time balancing accountability. When we hire young associates, their parents should be able to expect that our managers who guide them are going to teach them the things we believe in–character, values and ethical behavior. That's why we're in business.

So when bad things happen–things that go against the grain of everything we believe in–we're going to make it right. I remember a situation where an individual in a high level position unexpectedly asked those who reported to him to write the names of those they would let go if it were required (one wrote his own name down three times).

This leader purposely put his people into a state of fear (for their people). And even though his results had been positive up to that point, it was important to let every associate working for us know that we will always do the right thing by each and every one of them. There was no other choice and the person he reported to made the decision that was aligned with our principles. This leader had to become a part of our alumni.

Traditional HR can get so caught up in protecting against lawsuits that they stop showing care and compassion, taking the "human" out of human resources. Don't get me wrong, there is a lot of responsibility and liability we have to account for every day—that's just a fact of doing business anywhere and attorneys can be helpful partners. In buying or selling a company and other business related matters their advice can be invaluable.

But when it comes to people, they cannot be the "face" of the company, nor should they ever be used as an excuse for not doing the right thing. Devastating and tragic things can also happen in any business. We had a driver in Indianapolis who had an epileptic episode, ran a red light, and hit a car driven by a husband with his wife who was pregnant with twins. It was a terrible situation, but we got in a car and immediately drove to meet the families at the hospital. The twins were fine, but the woman and husband had complications, as did our driver, who ended up partially paralyzed as a result of the accident.

Another incident involving a delivery driver took the life of a young woman. And again, we drove straight to see the family. Many attorneys advise their clients to stay put and ride out the situation to avoid potential legal implications. Keeping the lawyers in perspective, they are focused on protecting the company, and I understand and respect that. But every time it comes down to a choice between doing the safe thing (nothing or "no comment") and doing the right thing (meeting the people where they are), there's never a

question of what our people are going to do.
For example, There was a horrible situation that
occurred in one of our stores in Indianapolis. No
bodily harm was done, but the pain was just as
real. We had a new manager-in-training working
his very first shift on a Sunday afternoon. A group
of girls and their adult group leaders came in,
hoping to have a party in the party room. There
were too many girls to be accommodated in the
room, which had an occupancy limit. New in his
job and trying to do things by the book, he dug in
his heels and said, "he couldn't serve them."

This group happened to be African-American
and shortly after the incident they filed a class-
action lawsuit against Donatos for refusing
to serve them. While I don't believe that the
manager had a discriminatory bone in his body,
he made a real mistake. At the time McDonald's
owned us and I was advised to "let the attorneys
handle it." Leaving it to the lawyers made us very
uncomfortable. My brother and I insisted we just
go to meet with them so that we could explain
who we are and help them understand that this
was an honest mistake.

We went to meet with the group of girls and their parents. We weren't quite prepared for the anger we encountered, but we immediately empathized with the parents of these nine-year-old girls and how wrong it must have felt to be turned away from our restaurant. We went to work repairing our relationship with these girls. Over the course of a year, we attended their group's meetings and talked to them about what we could do differently as a company. We ended up incorporating some of their ideas into our policy manual.

Eventually the lawsuit was dropped, but more important to us was the fact that these girls and their parents and leaders forgave the mistake and fell in love with Donatos again. The fan letters we received from some of those girls are among my most treasured mementos of my Donatos experience. It takes time to rebuild trust in any relationship, but the effort is unquestionably worth it.

I understand that it's easier and safer to push a complicated matter on to an attorney to handle. Your attorney's job is to protect the company. But as my dad has advised, when you give resistance, you get resistance back. Instead of resisting, take the sometimes painful learning experience as a gift–don't give it resistance–and you will find it opens a whole world of opportunity and something good will come out of it.

PEOPLE-FIRST RELATIONSHIPS

If you asked my dad, what frustrated him about our relationship is that I am slower than he is to implement or execute. I need to take the time to be sure that people understand and buy in to an idea or a decision, and that they feel that we've reached that point together. Once my dad has landed on an idea or decision, he's immediately saying, "Is it done yet? Is it done yet?"

This was partly due to the rather distinct differences in our personalities. Taking the Myers-Briggs Type Indicator (MBTI) together helped to identify the different ways my dad and I have always approached things. My MBTI type preference is ENFJ (extroverted, intuitive, feeling, judging), while my dad's is ENTP (extroverted, intuitive, thinking, perceptive). Over time, our differing approaches brought balance to our relationship and to our relationships with our people.

In my opinion, the Chief People Officer establishes the standard for relating to the people (a feeling preference) within the organization and must also represent that standard on the executive team. That can take additional time. I believe my dad supported me in my role because it so clearly reflects the values he's held (an intuitive preference) for 50 years about providing an environment where folks can bring their principles to work.

With either approach, our company's emphasis has always been on building people-first relationships. But, I remember our belief having a little wake-up call after McDonald's acquired Donatos. I had been out on maternity leave just after the acquisition, and when I returned to work there were 28 new executives–all VPs–ensconced in the home office.

I went office-to-office to introduce myself, doing the usual on-boarding, relationship building with these new associates; inquiring about their roles in the company, asking if they've had their drug tests, etc. The more I spoke with these new people, the more I began to realize that the swift addition of so many people coming from McDonald's and other companies had happened with little indoctrination into the Donatos way.

These were great people with terrific credentials, but I realized that I had failed at ensuring a proper relationship building, on-boarding experience for them. That's when we created the "Our Promise" class to introduce all new associates to the Donatos people-first way and to our core people-focused values. It's funny for me to think about it now. I was nervous, feeling that what I was saying seemed like the "soft stuff" to them.

That's when I realized that it would take time to build relationships and merge our cultures without losing our spirit and soul. In a symbolic way, I actually started charging a dollar for every time someone said "franchisee" instead of "franchise partner" or "royalty" instead of "licensing fee" or "employee" instead of "associate." One year we collected $2,500 just from meetings and day-to-day conversation, with the money going straight to our goodwill committee to donate to charity.

Of course I understood that the McDonald's team and other industry executives had used the term "franchisee" for 30 years in an industry where that was the custom. But when people refer to "franchisee," they project a message about the relationship–that our franchise partners would be treated as franchisees have been historically treated in our industry–and that simply wasn't true. When you call someone a partner, she acts like a partner. When you call her a franchisee, she acts like a participant in a transaction.

Many of the people in the Donatos family have been with us for a long time–20, 30, even 40+ years. Like me, most have grown up literally in the pizza shop and have learned our people-first approach to relationships. We hope that every person we hire, whose character and skills we help to develop, will stay with us forever, as so many of our folks have done.

But the fact is, if you're doing your job right, you're helping people grow their skills and self-confidence to the point where they want to realize their own goals and dreams. We believe that whether people are with us for a short term or long term, our job is to make sure that their relationship with us was one of goodwill.

And even though we were ultimately not able to effectively merge our cultures, I hope the McDonald's people would say the same thing. That it was a relationship of goodwill. ♥

BRIAN CRUMLEY
Franchise Partner, S&C Restaurants, Inc.–*A family culture that impacts lives*

"Our culture at Donatos is a family culture that has impacted many lives. In my 20 years with the company I have seen a lot of terrific people come and go, especially the kids. While it may be 'just a high school job' for these young associates, we always expect them to go on to bigger and better things, whether within our company or someplace else.

Everyone remembers their first boss, good or bad, and I always try to keep that in mind with these kids; that we're the ones making the first impression on them. That's why it's so important to treat them with respect, because you're showing them the value of treating others with the respect that you hope they will take into their future jobs.

I've been with Donatos since I was a kid myself. I started at 16, and by 19 I was a general manager responsible for several stores, including a new store in Canal Winchester for which we had extremely high expectations. One day about a year after it opened, I was in the store and a young associate named Lisa asked if I had a minute to sit down and talk to her. Of course, I agreed to speak with her, and what she said has stuck with me to this day.

She told me that there was an assistant manager there that was directing the associates to skimp on toppings in order to keep food costs down and show higher profits for the store. She said that she believed Donatos had the best products and that she was very proud to serve her home community our products. But if it was the company's plan to come to town and serve great products for a year, then start to skimp on the ingredients in order to increase profits, she didn't want to be a part of it any longer.

She understood that we weren't serving pizzas, we were serving people—in her case, the people of her hometown. Our conversation made me realize that everything we do in our stores has

Continued on page 216

Continued from page 215

an impact on those communities, including the local folks who work there, and as business leaders in these communities, every day we have a choice of whether that is a positive or negative impact. I have always been grateful to Lisa for making me understand that the associates are serving the people from their own neighborhoods, and that Donatos could make an important contribution to these communities.

Look, there's a chance that the kid you just hired could become the President of the United States–a small chance, I know, but still a chance. That's why we have do the right thing in the way we conduct our business and treat them with respect, so they'll go on to do the right thing and treat others with respect in whatever leadership roles they might have in the future. This world can be a much better place, and if it has to start in a pizza shop, so be it."

CHAPTER 4
PROSPERITY

I can remember Dad talking about prosperity from the very beginning of our business. He was taught at The Ohio State University that to produce goods and services for the sole purpose of making a profit was good business. A lot of business classes teach that. But, as stated earlier, dad always struggled with that concept. He believed the purpose should be so much greater and that's when he started talking about prosperity. It's important to be profitable, but it's more than just making a profit. It's what you do with that profit. It's how you reinvest in people and the community. It's a holistic approach.

We believe that prosperity is really the "soul" purpose of being in business. Prosperity means having a healthy body, mind, spirit and emotions, and that encompasses the business. It's important to be profitable so a business can prosper. Using the word profit has so many negative connotations. People associate it with big corporations and feel that it's bad or evil.

So the ideal of prosperity is important–to make a profit so that you can do good things with the money. Dad always said, "Good people can do great things with money, so good people should make money."

There is a difference between the words prosperous and profitable. When people think of profit they think of money that drops to the bottom of the balance sheet after all of their hard work, directly into the pockets of the owners. The word profit itself sounds hard. Prosperous is about the entire company's and person's well being. Money goes back into the business, goes back to help people grow, to help other people in the organization and the community. It's abundance, allowing people to grow and develop as individuals in our company.

When you ask the average person how much profit Donatos makes on a $10 pizza they might say $10 or $5 or something less. It ends up all the way down at the bottom–the "bottom line." But prosperity means that you put money back into the business, you pay people, you provide them training. You make sure that your buildings are assets to your neighborhood. You're a good neighbor, and you give back.

That's why prosperity is an important part of our business. You have to make money in order to give back, in order to pay people, in order to be better, in order to develop others. Getting away from what it is in the dictionary. Getting away from the fact that it's viewed as a bad word. Profit is not a bad word and it shouldn't have negative connotations associated with it. As my good friend Margie Pizzuti, CEO Columbus Goodwill Industries, states, "With no margin there is no Mission". It's the energy and what you do with it. Profit is what feeds prosperity. You need an organization that's alive. You need a mission. Prosperity is the purpose and profit is the fuel.

Recently my son, Tony Capuano, gave me an entirely new perspective on the definition of business. He stated that Webster's Dictionary may, in fact, be defining business with the actual intention of goodwill, and that perhaps it is our society who has been incorrectly interpreting "exchanging money for goods or services." He taught me that maybe the "services" are meant to be for the good of the people and not just tangible objects. It is interesting to note how different generations have different perspectives on the art of doing business. Maybe it is bigger than the words by which we define ourselves after all.

My son is pursuing a social enterprise opportunity where the profits of his business are for the sole purpose of giving back through his services.

CELEBRATING OUR PAST EXPERIENCE

From the early days, Dad visualized Donatos as being in business for 100 years and beyond. That's how we made our decisions, for long-term prosperity. But we did take time beginning in 2013 to celebrate our 50th anniversary along with Dad's birthday. It was a special time and a time to reflect on the next 50 years and beyond.

At the beginning I noted that writing this book took longer than I expected, and celebrating our 50th anniversary and the events that followed were some of the reasons my writing was delayed. The gatherings gave our entire Donatos family a chance to look back at how far we have come.

One of the most memorable events for me was an alumni party we threw at the Center Of Science and Industry (COSI). We invited all the Donatos alumni to join us for free pizza and to enjoy the evening with our CEO's band, Grassinine. We were there to celebrate. Obviously, our immediate family members were there along with the people that worked for us over the years. We couldn't believe the number of alumni who attended. They came back to Columbus from everywhere. Some drove across states to get here. The greatest part of the evening was the connection between people. It's what I think is so strong about a family, or a business that has family in it.

People had not seen each other for years, but as soon as they did the great stories and memories started flowing. People kept talking about their times together at Donatos. They came with their families to reconnect with our family. To me it was so impactful. It made me realize how important our "people-first" approach has been with the alumni and will continue to be with our current associates, many who have been with us for as many as 45 years!

People coming back were such great examples of the connection and the shared goodwill. Even

THE MISSING PIECE Jane Grote Abell

people that were asked to become alumni came back. As mentioned earlier, our goal has always been that if we say goodbye to people, their experience with us was one of goodwill–to have them write us a letter and say thank you for the experience here and that they learned something. We have received letters from people over the years and more letters came from people who attended the event.

We also had people come back that had only been with us for a short period of time. Yet however long or short their time was, Dad seemed to know most of them by name and could share stories with them. They seemed bound together by a common energy. It was a group of people who had been connected by a common thread, our mission and promise.

At the same time, people in our communities were expressing their appreciation. We assume that many companies get the customary proclamations, but we were overwhelmed by the heartfelt thanks we received. People didn't just present, or read to us, their proclamations–they added their own personal stories and thanked us for being a key part of their communities. They really knew who we are, our principles, and our commitment to the people and neighborhoods we serve. We could feel that our message was being heard. It was beyond anything we had expected.

Donatos associates celebrating the 50th anniversary.

UNDERCOVER BOSS

I have always found it interesting that our family business has gotten so much national attention from our competitors and other industry icons. The example I mentioned earlier was in 1996 when Pizza Hut conducted an entire research project, Project Woody, dedicated to trying to figure out what makes us different. They copied our trademark "Edge to Edge" and expanded their version of our pizza "The Edge" nationwide. My father always said that imitation is the sincerest form of flattery.

Another example was the McDonald's acquisition in 1999. While we were always looking to expand the business based on principles, we certainly never imagined that we would catch the eye of the world's largest restaurant company. We have been blessed with a lot of opportunities to gain regional and national exposure, but never did we think we would be selected for a national reality television episode of *Undercover Boss.*

Tom Santor, Executive Director of Public Relations, received a phone call in late November 2012 from a producer for the show *Undercover Boss* on CBS inquiring whether or not we would be interested in appearing for the show. I was a fan of the show and I was always inspired by how many people were able to change their lives as a result of their experience. As our President and CEO Tom Krouse says, "You say yes until there is a reason to say no," so we jumped into this one with a little hesitation.

They were looking for a female executive and the opportunity to film a pizza restaurant. Our first reaction was to listen and explore the opportunity with an open mind. We recognized immediately the opportunity to be able to help people in our company. But we also recognized the vulnerability and risk there would be by participating in the show.

I remember vividly that cold December day when we received the official invitation to appear on *Undercover Boss* for an episode in the Fall of 2013. While we were excited to have the opportunity, I have to admit that I was more nervous than excited.

Our discussions immediately moved to a series of questions and identifying "worst case scenarios." We are friends with the family of White Castle, so we enlisted their input regarding the show.

White Castle is a third generation family business in Columbus, Ohio. They were featured in the first season of *Undercover Boss*. In addition, we called a few other CEOs who had participated in the show and, hands down, each one of them said that it was a life changing experience and they would do it again. They stated that it was exhausting, but worth the time they put into the experience.

While we were moving forward with "say yes until there was a reason to say no", we were not finding a lot of reasons to say no. Although we did talk about potential things that could happen on the show that could possibly put our family business in a bad light. We were concerned with how our franchise partners would respond once they knew we were exposing the company nationally. We were concerned that we couldn't tell anyone anything and that meant our Donatos family and our franchise partners.

We were, however, confident in our people and their passion for our product, so we were not concerned that our people or our product would be compromised on the show. What we didn't know was the unimaginable–we had no idea that we would uncover such a controversial subject. Obviously this was one of the risks.

Participating in the show meant that we had to give up all creative and editorial rights. We would not be able to preview the show prior to it airing on national television. We had to give our total selves to the process and trust that our people would shine, that we would learn something new, and that we could help some well deserving people at the end of the show.

Weighing all the pros and cons, we immediately recognized two substantial opportunities. First and foremost was the opportunity to help people in a way that we would not normally be able to do by assisting them financially and in life in general. The sole purpose of *Undercover Boss* is to expose issues for the company so they can improve the work environment and the lives of the individuals in the show.

Shortly after we committed to *Undercover Boss*, a number of staff from the show came to Columbus

to meet with associates in our restaurants
for what was a ruse–a documentary on "the
restaurant industry". Tom Santor, our Executive
Director of Public Relations, was committed to the
entire process.

When we were given permission to let our family
members in on the show, it all became a little bit
more real. I think that is when I started to panic.

But we were not allowed to tell anyone outside of
our close circle that we would be on the show. My
family was completely and totally supportive of
the show and encouraged us to just "be present"
during the experience. We all agreed that the
founding principles of our family business would
shine through no matter what we encountered.

After participating in the entire process, I have to
admit I really respect the way the reality show is
made, both the selection process and the show.
I walked away from this experience a better
person, and I believe more in the show today than
ever before. Make no doubt about it, it's intense. It
is emotionally, mentally and physically draining.

For a little over a week, we spent each day getting make-up, working in the store, and doing before and after interviews. My disguise was quite elaborate, it took 1.5 - 2 hours to make me up every day, fixing my wig and ensuring I was in character at all times.

Personally, I struggled with two issues; one, being away from my family and secondly, pretending to be someone I wasn't. Even though some of my days would be here in town, I had to stay at a hotel so that I wasn't walking in and out of my house as my other identity. My alter-ego was "Cathy" and my disguise was "rock-a-billy". I had a black wig, brown contacts, tattoos, nose rings and an overall different persona. I didn't know where I was going. I didn't know where I would be staying.

Walking into a store and pretending to be someone else was totally against my core. But once we got started, I realized how much we could help people by working on the front line again—working the drive thru, the counter, making pizzas, marketing and delivering pizzas with our people who make a difference every day.

What a blessing to be able to work beside these people who had no idea who I was and could tell me anything without fear. It felt weird but my purpose was to be part of the crew out front. It wasn't about me. It was really about helping people.

Going into *Undercover Boss,* we realized that we just needed to have trust. Our Donatos name was out there for everyone to see. More importantly, we totally trusted our people. We knew they could have filmed all 5,000 of our associates and we would be confident that they would have found an inspiring story from everyone of our family members.

Our first stop was in Virginia with Buffy. I remember walking into the store repeating my name "Cathy" in my head a million times so I wouldn't say, "Hello, my name is Jane". Immediately Buffy's personality radiated and I knew she was serious about her job and cared about her team. She was a manager of the restaurant and her role was to train me on making pizzas and building sales through local store marketing. Her personality was contagious.

Photo Courtesy of Studio Lambert

Dressed as Cathy on Undercover Boss.

Buffy trained me on the importance of using scales, quality products and corrected me when I made the Founders Favorite wrong. Yes, I actually made my dad's favorite pizza without a key ingredient, the banana peppers. I appreciated the fact that she not only corrected me, she shared with me how important it is that I take the time to make the product right. She told me that the founder's mission was to treat others the way you want to be treated and to make sure that the customer got what they paid for. She told me the constraints of our web ordering system and how improvements could better serve the customers.

As I got to know Buffy over the next eight hours, she also shared with me her personal story. She was a manager of a hotel when one of her employees was shot and killed. She had a difficult time dealing with the situation and eventually moved away from the area. She lost contact with her children and was not able to maintain stable work until Donatos. We were able to help Buffy reconnect with her children and offered housing for her along with a promotion to become the general manager of the restaurant.

Then we had the opportunity to meet Kanisha!
I will never forget walking into the store I
used to manage and asking for Kanisha. I was
immediately impressed with her smile and energy.
Kanisha's energy and enthusiasm for her job was
outstanding. I easily gravitated to being with
her as she trained me in every step of the front
counter. She continued to reinforce that she
would be right beside me to guide me and help me
through the training on the computer. This store
had our new computer system so it was a little
easier to train me on taking orders.

After a few hours Kanisha and I had the
opportunity for some down time. While we folded
boxes she shared with me her story about her
family. I was completely shocked to hear her tell
about the loss of her brother and the hard times
that she has overcome. She was simply inspiring.
Kanisha has overcome more in her 18 years than
most people will face in a lifetime.

We had the opportunity to help Kanisha with a car
and cash but more importantly we were able to
do a promotion with Donate For Life. She wanted
to ensure that the legacy of her brother Taylor

lived on. He passed away at a young age, playing basketball, due to a heart condition he had from birth. She wanted to make sure that she was able to keep Taylor's legacy.

What I most love about this young woman is the selfless love she has for her family. She has accomplished so much but wants to make sure that his legacy is carried on for generations to come. I am proud to say that she is attending college and studying biology and pre-med. She is VP of Housing for her sorority and participating in two missionary trips in the upcoming months. She is truly inspiring!

Then I had the opportunity to meet Tangee. As I walked into the store I asked for Tangee and she introduced herself to me immediately. She had a quiet polite personality, but it was clear she expected a lot of me during our training experience. She wasn't going to put up with a lack of knowledge on my part. She took pride in her work, but struggled with training me on the "old computer" system. She was surprised that I wasn't picking up on things and was frustrated with me during our eight hours together.

At first, I found it hard to connect with Tangee. My personality was a little over-bearing for her and yet as I watched her with her customers I was impressed with the care and attention she took. She was training me on the drive up window. She knew her customers, she laughed with them, and she knew what they ordered before they even told her what it was. That evening, we had a chance to clean up the dining room and that is where I got to see a little more of Tangee.

What a beautiful soul–a young lady who never had the experience of being a teenager. She had to grow up well beyond her years and take responsibility for finances to make ends meet at home. She and her mom were making ends meet but truly living paycheck to paycheck. We had the opportunity to help by paying bills, tuition and a car. My favorite experience was going with Tangee to get her temps!

And then, I walked into our campus store to meet Aaron. A few things happened during my visit at this location. When I walked in our manager Kim recognized me immediately. I knew as soon as she looked me up and down that she knew who I was, so I pulled her aside and asked her to work with me on the "ruse". She was the ultimate professional and willing to do whatever we needed to assist in the goal of finding out how we could make the company an even better place to work.

She went back to work and rallied the associates to focus on the right things while I introduced myself to Aaron. Aaron was the perfect driver, one we would want to utilize as a role model. He was all about being safe, on time, the accuracy of the order and customer service. He literally timed me from the car to the door and back again to ensure that I had a sense of urgency.

And then it happened. Late into the night around 1:00 a.m., Aaron decided to tell me that he sometimes smokes pot with his customers while he is delivering pizzas. I cannot explain my reaction properly on paper. I was shocked, dismayed, angry and confused all at the same time. While we drove back to the store, I moved into "Mom mode" and started lecturing him on why his decision was not a good decision. Ultimately, we had to make a decision on what to do.

Here is this great kid who was doing all the right things for our customers, but he decided that it was OK to smoke pot with our customers on delivery. This put us at risk! It happens to be illegal in the state in which we are doing business and it isn't the best use of his time while he is working.

It was a bad night when I went back to the hotel room. I didn't know how my decision to act with Aaron was going to come off to the world, but I knew in my heart what we would do to help make a positive out of a negative situation. I knew that we would do the right thing by giving it 24 hours to make the decision. It ultimately meant firing him. We had to make a statement that it isn't OK to use legal or illegal drugs while delivering pizzas for our family business.

We had to let Aaron go, but we told him that if he passed a drug test in 30 days he could come back to work in the kitchen, and after another drug test he could go back out on deliveries to make more money. He has now passed six drug tests and is working for us during his last year and earning his degree. I am proud of Aaron for sticking through the tragedy of the situation, being so public about it, and working toward a better life. He is a great guy!

We are blessed. We have received so many positive messages about the appearance on *Undercover Boss* and how our mission came across. Everyone had a story. We put together a book of over 5,000 email comments.

I was overwhelmed by the responses from all over the world. One letter that stood out to me was from a solider named Rob. Rob grew up on the south side of Columbus near our first store. He actually saw the episode, while serving in Afghanistan. He said that he was reminded of home and what he was fighting for. When he returned to the United States, he sent us a package.

US EMBASSY, KABUL AFGHANISTAN

Presents This Flag To
JANE ABELL

This is to certify that the accompanying flag of the
United States of America was flown in the face of
the enemy over the US Embassy, Kabul
Afghanistan by the Officers, NCOs
and Airmen of the 466th Air Expeditionary
Group during Operation
ENDURING FREEDOM on the
23d day of August, 2014.

MICHAEL J. EPPER, Maj, USAF
966 Air Expeditionary Squadron
Deputy Commander

Inside was a beautifully folded American flag. It was the flag that flew over the US Embassy in Kabul, Afghanistan. I was incredibly touched.

People all around the world have now heard of the Donatos Mission. That is well worth any risk or reward situation.

ADMITTING MISTAKES

In many ways the *Undercover Boss* experience was a test of how far we have come over the last 50 years. And before our year of celebration was over we had another significant test. This one was unexpected. It came on Tuesday, July 22nd, 2014, when our phones started "blowing up." I received a text from one of our managers that said, "Please make it stop." Apparently a coupon was being presented for a free large pizza at our stores and it wasn't an approved coupon.

The coupon was supposed to be given to customers in one store in Cuyahoga Falls, Ohio, who signed up for the email club. We had just spent two months promoting it. But, an error occurred and it is hard to understand how it happened. It resulted from flipping a "switch" in the system. The coupon went viral and live in all our restaurants. Our managers didn't know what to do, but made the decision on their own that the right thing to do was to accept the coupon. We'll investigate later but the right thing to do was to accept it.

We tried to turn it off, but instead it was turned on in the entire system. At the same time it went viral and then exponential, as people were copying and sending the coupon to others. Over the course of the next four to five hours, 16,000 free pizza coupons were being redeemed and our stores and our people were overwhelmed. Five stores had to be shut down because they ran out of food. People were tailgating in our parking lots. There were crowd and safety concerns.

Tom Pendery, our COO, met with the team all night determining our next steps. First, we were going to apologize. Secondly, we knew the media was all over the story and we needed to better understand what happened. That's another thing

TOM KROUSE
President and CEO, Donatos Pizza–
We apologized

"Through the chaos there were also people trying to order and they were having trouble getting pizzas. We ended up collecting names and phone numbers of 2,300 customers that were affected. We had them in our system. People were puttng orders in for the next day for free pizzas. We had a group of around 12 people call up each and every one of them the next day to explain what happened and say that we apologize. We didn't totally roll over. We told them we did not intend to give out free pizzas.

Some of the people knew they had a coupon that was not valid. When we called them to apologize they said–'I had a feeling, it's fine, thank you.' Some of them wanted to go back to the store and pay them for the pizza. I think internally having our home office associates call those customers validated what we did and increased how much our customers appreciated it. We screwed up. We apologized."

we have learned, to be open to the media. If the media asks questions, answer the questions. So we did. We were just trying to help customers understand that the universal free coupon was not intentional.

We apologized! Our managers and associates are the ones that got the brunt of it. There were mobs of people and it was stressful on our people. Working days like that, there's nothing fun about it. It was also about apologizing to the customer who really just wanted to feed her family that day and was going in to buy a pizza and never got her dinner.

Social media can cause a PR crisis but it also brought our people together. Our managers were thanking associates who came from other stores to help out. They created an energy–"we got hit hard–but thank you." There were some skeptics who were saying, "It's a big company trying to cover their butts for something they did on purpose." But there were other customers defending us. We even had alumni on Facebook defending us saying, "We know Donatos and there's no way that it would have been a marketing scam."

It was heartwarming. I think the most powerful thing about a crisis is how you operate, what's your core, your reaction? Although Tom Krouse and I were the most visible to the public, Tom Pendrey, our Chief Operating Officer, had "our back." He was up 24 hours straight monitoring Facebook and the media. He owned it. He had only been here a little over six months at the time. It's another example of making sure you align the right people with your values.

In a follow-up meeting, Tom Pendrey pointed out how the "free pizza" affected our franchise partners. He said, "We need to reimburse them for their labor and the food." It had cost us a lot in our company stores and he was adding to our loss. But he wasn't afraid to say, "Absolutely, we're doing it." It is the right thing to do!

TOM PENDREY
COO, Donatos Pizza–
We owned it

"I started at Donatos in January of 2014. Prior to that I had been vice president and general manager of the Gross & Jarson Pepsi Cola Bottling Company in Columbus and knew both Jane Abell and Tom Krouse and had admired them for how they had kept the company going through the recession. They bought the company back from McDonald's in 2004 and shortly after that, beginning in 2006, the economy went bad. It was a tough time for all of us in the food and beverage businesses.

When I came to Columbus I had my first Donatos pizza and I really liked it. And by knowing both Jane and Tom I knew about their principles. Like them, I had spent my entire career emphasizing the importance of the customer. So when I had the opportunity to come to Donatos, I took it. Little did I realize how soon and how significantly my belief in the customer would be tested.

It's ironic, but the day (July 22nd) began with a Town Hall meeting where I emphasized the importance of building customers. It wasn't until late afternoon when our people from marketing stopped by my office that I got my first hint of the problem that was unfolding. There was a mistake with a coupon from the Cleveland area. We made the decision to accept it, thinking that maybe 100 to 200 people had it and a few dozen might redeem it.

After a long day I went home and shut off my phone not realizing a groundswell was building truly exponentially. By 7:00 pm it went viral. When I finally picked up my phone and saw what was happening I stayed on the phone throughout the night. We were determining our next steps, what to do in the morning. In the meantime, the people in our stores were dealing with it. They had a choice. They could have become grumpy, or they could do it and have fun. Everybody jumped in.

Our system was handling it, but our on-line ordering had to be shut down. People couldn't get through on the phone so they were coming

Continued on page 246

Continued from page 245

to the stores. Our lots were flooded with people. The police came to direct traffic. Many of our people worked through the night to be ready in the morning. We restocked all the stores that were impacted. We were all living our mission and our promise.

When we couldn't fulfill the promise we could see it in the system (late deliveries, pizzas not ready on time). We knew we had to deal with it directly to gain our credibility and respect back. The next day a team of associates contacted customers to make it right. Jane apologized to our customers on our web site and I apologized to our associates and franchise partners. We owned it.

We compensated our franchise partners–they didn't have to ask. Some wanted to know whose fault it was. We said we don't have time to determine that now–first we have to make it right. I have always said–don't measure me by what I say, measure me by what I do. I couldn't be prouder of our people. I would do it all, all over again."

THE NEXT 50 YEARS

As my dad said, "Prosperity is longer term and inclusive. It means the well being of everyone–our people, our customers and those we do business with." I think if you ask any organization about its future, the people will say that growing is part of their plan. Growth often drives their mission. But Donatos is different. Our mission drives our need to grow. It is part of our Destiny–*To be a principle-based, profitable company dedicated to our Mission and Promise for 100 years and beyond.*

And growth is embedded in our Philosophy–*To Live, Love, Laugh and Learn–There is always a better way to learn, grow, stretch–keep moving forward.* That means the best thing for Donatos is to grow. It's because we believe that the mission, destiny and promise of our company has a very positive impact on the community we serve, our customers and our people. Our growth fuels our prosperity.

It starts with our quality brand delivered by happy associates and franchise partners supported by world-class systems–our operating system, our people system, accountability system, and the management tools that we are putting into place. But we are not just a manufacturer that makes quality pizza and has people taking orders. It's people that understand serving others with a servant leadership. That's the epitome of our brand.

FRANCHISING

We are continuing to grow our restaurants and enter into new markets primarily through our franchise partners. Franchising is interesting because some will say it takes away from an organization. But for us it is a way to build on our core competency and leverage what happens in the restaurants. I had first hand experience of understanding the power of franchising when Dad and I bought back the company and I signed the front of the check instead of the back. As a franchise partner you aren't just investing in a

restaurant, you are investing in the "recipe",
the philosophy, the mission, the promise and
the destiny.

TIM YOUNG
**Director Franchise Operations,
Donatos Pizza–*Working backwards***

*"I started at Donatos in 1979, a few months after
my brother Todd. We consider ourselves the '2nd
generation,' after Jim, Willy, Donice and Roger.
I think I was the first official manager in
training, opening the campus store when I was
21. When the training department started I
moved there with Charlene Rose and later Jane.
That's when I created the curriculum for the
manager in training program.*

*I am more linear in my thinking and like to start
with the end in mind and work backwards. Now
that I am in franchising I think the same way,
working backwards identifying what's needed*

Continued on page 250

Continued from page 249

to open a new store, or a new market. Our role is as business consultants, helping our franchise partners grow sales and profits.

Others may see franchising operations as more of an inspection role. We see ourselves as brand ambassadors, setting and repeating our high standards. That's the key, high expectations and accountability, along with treating people with dignity and respect. We influence people's lives by what we do. When I go into a new restaurant, I ask myself, 'Would I want my grandkids to work here?' If the answer is no–we fix it.

It all starts with picking the right people to be franchise partners. We look for people who want to be mentored. It's part of our vetting process, looking for like-minded people. It's personal to me. This is my family. I see us building a legacy–100 years and beyond. That's the end state–we are working backwards from there."

But you are not buying the actual part that makes it work, which is the person—the franchise partner. As our CEO Tom Krouse says, "You're the battery." Our franchise partners actually have to get involved, involved in the community, involved in the restaurant, involved with the people, thinking about making customers happy, making servers happy. You can't buy that. Because if you don't work at that restaurant, if you don't care about the people, if you let somebody else worry about it, it's just not going to be as successful.

Success is in the details, attention to the details. You have to care about all the people. You have to make sure that the birthday card you send gets there before the associate's birthday. You have to make sure that when people you care about come into your building that they are welcomed and greeted with a smile. It's about treating all people with respect. These are all important details.

Our franchise partners are our brand ambassadors. They deliver our quality products through happy associates supported by world-class systems. That's why selecting our franchise partners goes beyond a financial process to looking for and finding those who want to share in our destiny. Beyond serving more pizzas to more people, through more restaurants, delivered by more franchise partners, we will grow by exporting the solutions we create to solve our own problems to new markets and new customers. If you think about it that's what my dad did with the Pepp-A-Matic. He created it to solve his own problem of consistently slicing the pepperoni and then found new opportunities for marketing the equipment to others.

DIVERSIFIED PORTFOLIO

Shortly after buying our company back from McDonald's we had an opportunity to expand by adding Take & Bake pizzas in Kroger stores. Tom Krouse, with my father, led this strategy. But along with the opportunity came a new problem— how to "proof" the dough before sending it to the stores. We came up with the idea of our own central bakery where the dough could be made to our high quality standards and then shipped to our stores, along with Kroger, and ultimately other locations.

In addition to the need for more capacity in order to do take and bake, we needed to significantly change the cooking system and then other systems. And we needed new equipment. We needed new technology to be a state of the art bakery. Once again our own "Dr. Dough" Donice Foraker and Willy Webb found the way to make it all happen. We made a significant investment in this new concept, including about $12 million in a building and the equipment to allow us to be efficient.

We quickly recognized the potential for a new and different market opportunity, including private label products, and we also wanted to be able to sell to other pizza companies even if their crusts were different from ours.

We knew that it might send the wrong message to the public if our competitors were sourcing their dough from Donatos. Tom Krouse's brother Scott actually came up with the name "Jane's Dough" to identify the product as Jane's Dough, not Donatos pizza dough.

The growth of Jane's Dough continues along with the growth of the Grote Company. Like the Pepp-A-Matic, we started another company purely out of our preoccupation with making our product the best it can possibly be. Jane's Dough was born out of the idea that we need to guarantee that our Take and Bake pizzas absolutely reflect our same great quality.

DONATOS UNIVERSITY

From the earliest days of our company we recognized the importance of training to fulfill our mission, promise and destiny. Consistent with our philosophy–*a better way to learn, grow, stretch– keep moving forward*–we spend considerable resources training our people at all levels. The programs are taught by and embraced by our people. Much of the training, especially with our front line, is focused on the "why" we do what we do and then the "how" to do it with quality.

We also have a manager-in-training program, instituted in the late 70s when we had only a few restaurants. As mentioned earlier, my dad closed the first two stores he had opened (after the original one) when he encountered problems in assuring the consistency of our product. Training, and especially training new managers, was in response to the problem. We created our Promise class for all new associates to on-board them to our people centered culture. We believe our training opportunities and programs have set us apart from the rest of our industry.

Based on what we do and how we do it, Donatos has been featured, along with three other organizations, in a new book titled *We Leadership.* The belief is that when people say "we" at all levels it is a sign that they share in the mission, philosophy and goals of the organization. It is a simple way to determine if leadership is occurring and if people are engaged.

We have been encouraged to share what we do by opening our training programs to others. It would be another way of exporting the solutions we have created to solve our own problems to new markets and new customers.

HIRE PEOPLE SMARTER THAN YOU

As my dad emphasized when we first started growing our company in the 1980s, it's important to have the right people with the right skills in the right place. I know my strengths. I was a catalyst in the buyback and influential in the turn around but the future needed a different kind of leader. Now as we are growing in new ways and in new directions, I believe our CEO Tom Krouse is the right person to take us to the next level.

Tom was part of the talent we added during the time we partnered with McDonald's. Prior to joining us, he had been with Wendy's for almost a dozen years in key marketing positions, including Vice President of Marketing (where he oversaw a $140 million National Marketing Plan). His first position with Donatos was Senior VP of Marketing, but it was easy to see that his abilities and potential were much broader.

Tom is a great strategic thinker. He has an uncanny ability to see the big picture while at the same time making the complex seem simple to understand. As stated earlier when we were considering our options after McDonald's announced its intentions, Tom became a key part of the inner circle, what we called "the side." Even though there were no assurances that Tom would have a position when it was all over, he continued working throughout the process, providing his great insights and never wavering in his dedication.

After the buyback, Tom was critical in helping us plan for the future. He became our Chief Concept & Strategy Officer, leading many of our innovative efforts, while at the same time focusing on how we could become profitable through a slow but steady strategy. As we moved through the recession he played many important roles until he was named President & CEO in 2010.

In the last several years under his leadership, we have posted the highest profits in our company's history. Tom's "say yes until there is a reason to say no" approach guided us as we moved into new franchising development and the creation of Jane's Dough Foods.

It isn't all business with Krouse however. At work he is seen as a mentor, community activist and fun loving individual; as a singer/guitarist he performs with his bluegrass band Grassinine. He'll often surprise top performers by serenading them in the middle of meetings. Free-spirited camaraderie aside, Krouse means business– the last three years have shown positive sales outpacing industry trends. And Donatos has always been committed to giving back to the communities where we do business. Tom Krouse has truly taken this commitment to heart.

When we were meeting to discuss the title for this book, Tom quickly said, *"The Missing Piece."* He recognizes and understands how to merge the passion my dad has for the process and the product together with my passion for the people and our principles. He says his primary role as CEO is upholding the Mission and Promise through what he calls "a philosophy of performance" (results). And he does it in his own unique way–with APE, GOST, "Big Rocks" and a new twist on PIA.

Making the complex seem simple to understand,
Tom often uses acronyms. APE stands for Align,
Plan and Execute. Tom says APE is "floating over
our heads in meetings." Align means assuring what
we do is in alignment with our principles. Plan is
how to get there. Tom says, "Without a plan, it's just
a discussion." Then Execute. Tom adds, "Alignment
is a 'selfless' act." It requires "letting go" and his
advice is, "When you find yourself wanting to tell
people how to do it, stop and move your thinking
up a level." When you give up control, you get in
return "people who won't let you down."

GOST is another acronym. It's comprised of:
Goal, Objective, Strategy, Tactics & Timeline
(Measurement). While GOST reflects the "spirit"
of Donatos, the very visible side of our goals, our
process of owning as well as achieving them is
reflected in what Tom calls "Big Rocks." A Big Rock
is more than just a traditional organizational goal.
They are the "make or break" actions.

The "Big Rocks" focus on goals the associates
have agreed to, and they are communicated in

many different ways. If you walk around our offices you will see them in big posters on the walls in every department. Tom conducts one-hour "Big Rocks" meetings where the progress on each goal is reviewed in depth, problems discussed and, if needed, corrective actions identified.

Even though the meetings are scheduled to last one hour, each member of the leadership team clears their calendars for two hours. With the meetings, the prepared reports, the open discussions, the reports back to the departments from the team leaders, and the posters, the Big Rocks are aligned with our principles and owned not only by the leadership team but by each department and individual.

Here's what Tom Santor, our Executive Director of Public Relations, said about Tom in nominating him for *Columbus Business First's* C-Suite Award (Tom was selected as the Executive of the Year in 2014):

"I have heard Tom Krouse say, 'Love is the greatest energy one can put out. And I believe the more you put out, the more of it exists in the world, and the more you get back in return.'"

It is with this attitude that he lives each day. And for all these reasons and more, Tom and I married in 2015 and have blended our six children and started a new chapter in life and business.

OUR PROMISE AND MISSION

When Dad started the company, part of our promise was being a good neighbor. I remember it as a little kid, he would get upset if the person who was delivering would squeal his tires going down the alley because it would disturb neighbors on both sides of the restaurant. With Dad, it was always about making sure the restaurant was clean, the dumpsters were clean, no trash was lying around, and that the neighbors could take pride in the fact that the restaurant was literally in their backyard.

The important part of being a good neighbor is being an asset to the neighborhood. That meant we were always going to give back to the neighborhood. It meant picking up the trash that was in the alley. It meant that our lights weren't shining in their backyards keeping them up at night. It meant that our radio wasn't blaring so that it's bothering the neighbors. Even the location of our buildings was important because we were truly committed to being a good neighbor.

My entire life I've heard about "Our Promise." That's why being a good neighbor is so important to me. All of our stores have goodwill budgets so that they can sponsor the little league teams or sponsor the clean-up day or other events valued within their own neighborhood. Part of our local store marketing and training is about how you involve yourself in the community, how you go to the soccer games and sit in the bleachers and talk to the customers. Being a good neighbor always means conducting our business with respect for the community. Beyond that, it's about giving back and making a difference.

THE GOODWILL COMMITEE
–An inspiration

In 2005, Lori Haimerl, our Director of First Impressions, was inspired to organize her Donatos colleagues to give back. Since then, every January she sends around an email listing 10 or 12 charities and folks in the home office and the bakery vote for their top three choices. She then arranges for bake sales and raffles, with the money going to the chosen charities. In the first year of her efforts, the money went to the Ronald McDonald House, the Children's Hunger Alliance and the Mid-Ohio Food Bank. The people who contribute their time and effort to this work are known as the "Goodwill Committee."

For the first few years, the first three quarters of funds raised would go to the three chosen charities, and the fourth quarter funds might go to a Donatos family in need or to a class at

Continued on page 264

Continued from page 263

Southwood Elementary School. Donatos has developed a relationship with Southwood through Dorothy Smith, a 5ᵗʰ grade teacher who was the general manager of the downtown Columbus store before going into education.

Dorothy started pitching the Goodwill Committee to support her students whose families had financial challenges. Organized by Project Goodwill Coordinator Lori Haimerl, one of our holiday efforts has involved hanging ornaments that illustrate the needs and wishes of Dorothy's students (size M, loves Hello Kitty!) from the big Gift Tree at the home office. Donatos associates choose ornaments from the tree and provide gifts under the tree that are delivered to the students in Dorothy's class.

Recently, the Goodwill Committee decided to expand the reach of our holiday efforts to include the entire school by holding a "garage sale," where Donatos associates donate a variety of household items, toys, furniture, books, school supplies, candy and other items for Southwood families. Dorothy Smith reported that in 2013 more than 60 families had a holiday because of Donatos' truckloads of donations. She said she had prayed for 3,000 donations, but was amazed and grateful for the 7,000 donations that were delivered and made such an impact on her school community.

Approximately 85 percent of the Donatos family participates in Goodwill Committee giving activities. Some even participate in Southwood School Days, where students visit the home office and representatives from different departments talk to the students about what the company does, what work is like and what careers are open to them. They get a cool tour of the home office and bakery, and–of course– some great pizza.

LORI HAIMERL
Guest Services/Project Goodwill
Coordinator, Donatos Pizza–
Supporting the communites we serve

"Donatos has always been invested in supporting the communities it serves. The work of the Goodwill Committee is just one way Donatos' commitment to the community is expressed. Many of us were born and raised in these communities, so on a personal level it's deeply gratifying to be able to make a difference in the lives of children and families who are not just our customers, but are also our neighbors."

As Chairwoman of Donatos I have the blessing of spending most of my time on our philanthropic initiatives. Our most significant and most recent example of giving back is on the south side of Columbus where our business first began. I currently chair the board of Action for Children, a non-profit organization that focuses on advocacy for children and education. I joined the board in 2009 to learn from the former CEO, Diane Bennett. She is inspirational and the most intuitive and compassionate person I have had the pleasure of knowing. She is grounded in humility but radiates confidence.

As a part of serving on the board, I had an opportunity to visit a learning center located on the south side that has been there since 1928. This center was the first to support women who entered the workforce in the early 1900s. The center is a 5-star rated center where the staff are passionate and dedicated, but these little kids were in a building that was deteriorating.

We happen to live in a great city. Recently, Mayor Michael Coleman approached my dad and said, "You're from the south side and things have worked out pretty well for you. I need you to be a Champion for the south side."

The statistics in the neighborhood were dismal and deteriorating daily. In 2013 the child abuse was three times higher than any other area in the city and the unemployment rate was over 22 percent. Infant mortality is the third highest in the nation. One in four homes are boarded up. As we drove around the neighborhood with the Mayor and Janet Jackson, CEO of United Way, Dad would say, "I delivered pizzas to that house. I remember this community being a vibrant community. I remember people working. I remember people having perseverance and a great work ethic. What happened?"

It's not that people on the south side don't care anymore because they do, but the barriers they face have changed. They are not able to get past the barriers in front of them.

Out of that discussion, an incredible opportunity unfolded. As a family we contributed $1.5 million for what is now called the Reeb Avenue Center. My father's mentor, Don Kelly and his wife Nancy, who were already invested in the south side began to share their vision for doing something significantly different in the community. Don inspired us to go deeper to create real change. Don shared with our family the work that he was already doing to inspire change with early childhood learning and development by buying Dictionaries for the local third grade students every year. Don brought people together in his home to talk about real change. He started with the vision to 'go an inch wide and a mile deep' and not 'an inch deep and a mile wide". Don and Nancy have invested in the south side for many years, and recently contributed more than $500,000 to the Reeb Ave Center, and they lead the work with renovating and rebuilding lives with the Renaissance Housing Project.

Almost immediately, Tanny Crane and the Crane Family contributed $1 million to amplify the power of the private philanthropic dollars. This gift helped us to create a public/private partnership that will soon be recognized as a National Model. The Crane Group, founded in 1947, is a private holding and management company based in Columbus, Ohio. Their holdings comprise a network of local, regional and global companies in both manufacturing and the building trades. The Crane Group products and services are known for being innovative, high quality and backed by some of the strongest warranties in the industries they serve. They are a family-owned business, and celebrate and uphold the values, passion and drive established by its first generation's leadership. Tanny Crane serves as President and CEO and leads the strategy and direction of the organization with a people first culture. The Crane Group is much more than great product and services, they are about family, history and community.

Tanny Crane is one of the best examples of a balanced leader and I am proud to call her my mentor. She has taught me so much in life, personally and professionally. She is an exceptionally smart business leader, a great mom and my good friend. She is the perfect balance of a strategic leader who balances head and heart in business and in life.

Shortly after the vision was crafted, we brought on Kerri Laubenthal Mollard of Mollard Consulting to help us craft our vision and build a business plan to raise the funds to help our vision become a reality. Kerri Mollard has demonstrated the ability to articulate the vision, build a pro-forma, write a Request for Proposal for security and manage Tanny and myself. Tanny, Kerri and I have found our true labor of love, while giving tours of the Reeb Ave Center to over 100 potential donors in just 12-months.

Over the last year we had a number of generous donors help us raise $12.5 million to renovate the center. Our mission is to empower families through education and opportunity for workforce development. We aspire to create a pathway to prosperity. Since Reeb was an elementary school built in 1904, it has been serving the changing needs of its neighbors. Our construction goal is to restore the historic school to house more than a dozen nonprofit agencies, to renovate the multipurpose room for tenant and community use and to build a state of the art Early Learning and Development Center. All of which will holistically address the needs of the residents while celebrating the heritage of the community.

What I love most about this community is their love and pride for their neighborhood. The building has been vacant for over five years and the building stands with no graffiti, no broken windows and no vandalism. The Reeb Ave building was still equipped with TVs in every classroom and copper fixtures in the attic, and the building was never vandalized. We believe it's because the community sees it as their hub, their hub of hope.

We are putting education and lifelong learning at the core of the design. Our tenants and partners will create programs that teach and inspire from cradle through career to create opportunities, increase prosperity, and move the neighborhood forward from hungry to nourished.

Reeb Avenue Center is collaborative by design, as it will have intentional pathways between tenants so that each nonprofit can help to serve the holistic needs of every person who walks through the front door.

Our values are:

- **Lift Up -** Empower all with an inclusive environment of respect
- **Learning -** Education as fundamental to creating prosperity
- **Legacy -** Honoring the heritage of the south side and recognizing the achievements of the people and businesses who have called the south side home
- **Leadership -** Inspiring the next generation and fostering their growth and development
- **Love -** Caring deeply about our neighbors

The focus is on workforce development and education, a "hand up not a hand out."

Reeb was recently named one of "5 Nonprofits to Watch in 2015" by the Columbus Foundation, which honors innovative nonprofits poised for an exceptional year of growth and progress. And, the Association of Fundraisining Professionals (AFP) bestowed the highest honor to the Grote, Crane and Kelley families by awarding the "2015 Outstanding Philanthropist Award" for the exceptional generosity and leadership.

For more information on Reeb please visit www.reebavecenter.com.

So here we are, back where it all began-our old neighborhood-and we are giving back. It's like dad said about prosperity, "Our purpose should be so much greater. It's important to be profitable, but it's more than just making a profit, it's what you do with that profit. It is how you reinvest in people."

It really is the "soul" purpose of our being in business.

> **"Once a job has first begun, do it right until it's done."**
> 'Grandpa' Grote

Reeb Avenue Center forum scheduled for August

With the grand opening scheduled for this August, the former Reeb Avenue elementary school on the south side of Columbus will be transformed into a community resource. The center will be the topic of discussion at the CMC forum on Wednesday, Aug. 5 with panelists Tanny Crane from the Crane Group, Jane Grote Abell from Donatos and others involved in the project.

The concept will bring together successful partnering agencies to offer services to the neighborhood.

"Building a Hub of Hope" is their tagline but also the description of what makes this venture unique. The Reeb center will offer one location where nearby residents can find assistance for finding work, healthy meals, educational enrichment and training for children and adults and counseling services.

The participants in the center that work with school-aged children include Boys & Girls Clubs of Columbus and Eastway Behavioral Healthcare. COWIC/Ohio Means Jobs Franklin County, Godman Guild, St. Stephen's Community House, ConnectOhio and the Dawson Foundation will work with adults to provide resources to find or improve their employment opportunities.

The Mid-Ohio Foodbank and Community Development for All People will manage a "pay-as-you-can" café along with Lutheran Social Services that will manage a Benefit Bank. The City of Columbus South Side Neighborhood Pride Center will be present to offer answers to residents about City services. Finally, the South Side Learning and Development Center will move to the Reeb Center serving families' childcare and preschools needs.

The founders and supporters of the Reeb Center hope that the center will offer support to families and create greater self-sufficiency thereby strengthening the South Side neighborhood.

CMC forum panelists Jane Grote Abell and Tanny Crane in front of the new Reeb Avenue Center expected to open this August.

IT'S BIGGER THAN THE PIZZA—
EVERY PIECE IS IMPORTANT!

We believe love is shared when people gather around Donatos Pizza. We do what we love and we love what we do—and that is helping people share life's moments with great tasting pizza. We go to great lengths to make delicious pizza of the highest quality, but we think our job is bigger than that; it's to enhance the experience of getting together with family, friends and co-workers. It is to enrich peoples' lives and their relationships with one another. It's to build community. It's to think about people first—with Donatos pizza as a means to a bigger and much more fulfilling end.

Thinking back to Chapter 1, I said I didn't think of myself as a leader or an author. I said that I saw myself on a journey of becoming a leader. Little did I know then that writing this book would also become a journey, one where I learned more about my leadership, myself, and most importantly others.

As I wrote, I realized that I couldn't tell the Donatos story by myself. It became more about the family's story. At first it was the Grote family, but then it became the Donatos family as more and more associates joined with me in telling what became our story. The hardest part was selecting which stories to include. I thank all those who contributed and recognize there are many other stories our associates tell that aren't included.

Sadly, during the process of writing this book we have lost some very important Donatos family members. We lost them to heart failure, cancer and, most recently, one in a fatal accident while delivering a pizza. All of these individuals contributed to the fabric of Donatos. Whether they were with us for 30 years or six months, their presence made a difference in our family.

Dad said in his Foreword, his defining moment was when he realized that it is the people making the pizza that makes the difference. He stated that food served with love nourishes the soul. As our story unfolded we talked about our Product, our Principles, but most of all we told our story through our People. Discovering that the definition of Prosperity is really the "soul" purpose of our being in business.

Having a 'soul' in business isn't a new idea, but keeping your 'soul' while doing business is *The Missing Piece.* We recognize that the expression of our brand is merely a reflection of our people. We have the distinct honor of serving people with love and loving people who serve with their heart and soul.

We know and expect there will be more changes, those that are already underway as well as the uncertainty the future will bring along the way. But one thing is certain-our unwavering commitment to our principles-with *Character, Courage, Conviction and Compassion.*

> *"At Donatos we know it takes all the right ingredients to make something great, the right time, the right place, the right people and of course the right pizza"*

Every Piece is Important. ♥

PHOTOS FROM THE
DONATOS ARCHIVES

*Grandpa Grote in
uniform and with
Grandma Grote below.*

*My Grandpa and Grandma
Grote, Harold and Dorthy,
with Dad as a small child.*

Dad, Jim Grote, as a child.

My dad's high school graduation photo.

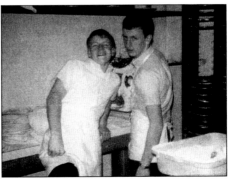

Donice Foraker and Roger Howard working at Donatos, circa 1968.

Our first menu at Donatos Pizza.

The Donatos crew at Thurman Avenue.

*Our original
3-wheeled
delivery vehicle.*

The Thurman Avenue Crew.

Dad with his truck he called "The Scout."

*My uncles–Larry Grote,
Dick Baumann and Hal Grote.*

*Grandpa and
Grandma Grote.*

Grandpa Grote on the right.

Grandpa Herman Baumann, Grandma Dorthy Grote, my mom, my brother Tom, my sister Katie and me, along with Grandma "TG" Baumann and Grandpa Grote.

Me with my Grandpa Baumann.

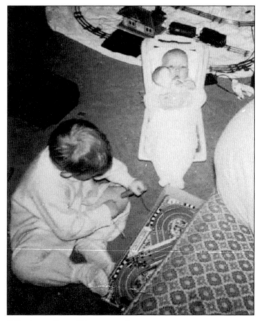

My brother Tom and me.

My Grandpa Baumann.

My brother Tom.

*Snapshots from
my childhood.*

*Here I am with my sister Katie and
my Aunt Nancy.*

*With my
brother Tom.*

*With my cousins, playing in my
Grandma Grotes' Basement.*

With my siblings
and my parents.

My first communion.

The Grote siblings at Christmas, Tom Grote, Jane Grote,
Katie Grote and Kyle Grote.

My first dog "Grouch" and my sister Katie.

Pictures from my childhood.

Here I am with Grandma TG, Katie, Tom, my mom and Grandpa Grote.

My sister Katie and me with TG.

High school dance team.

*With my dad just after we bought the company
back from McDonald's.*

With my mom (above) and Donice Foraker and Will Webb. In 2015, Donice and Will celebrated their 49th and 47th anniversaries with Donatos!

Throwing out the first pitch at the Columbus Clippers game. Shown (below) with Tom Krouse and Dad.

Roger Howard and Laura Fording.

Long time Donatos associates, Lianne McGlade and Roger Howard.

Donatos 50th Anniversary reunion.

With my lifelong friends from high school.

One of our "Stairway Welcomes" at the home office.

Tom Krouse with his band Grassinine.

With Buffy (above) and Kanisha (below) on Undercover Boss.

Kanisha with a photo of her late brother Taylor and after we bought her a new car following Undercover Boss.

*Photos
with Dad.*

Photo Courtesy of Kenneth Frick

With my husband Tom and our children, Kenny, Chaz and Joey Krouse, Tony Capuano, Brie and Tori Abell

Our Family.

PHOTOS FROM THE DONATOS ARCHIVES

THE MISSING PIECE   Jane Grote Abell

JANE GROTE ABELL
CHAIRWOMAN OF THE BOARD
DONATOS PIZZA

A founding family member of
Donatos Pizza, Jane Grote Abell
currently holds the title of
Chairwoman of the Board.

Over the last four decades, Jane has held a variety
of positions at both Donatos Pizza and Jane's
Dough Foods, Donatos' food service commissary
operations. In 1988, with a degree from Ohio State
University in Organizational Communications and
a strong passion for people, she was promoted
to Chief People Officer and served in this role
during the acquisition by McDonald's in 1999.
During the four years with McDonalds, Jane
served as Senior Vice President of Development
and maintained her role as Chief People Officer. In
these leadership positions, she helped steer the
company's business strategy. In 2003, Jane was
a major catalyst behind the decision to purchase
Donatos back from McDonald's. Following the
buyback, in December of 2006, Jane was promoted
to President and Chief Operating Officer.

Though Jane is heavily focused on the chain's mission of promoting goodwill through product, service, principles and people, since taking over as Chairwoman of the Board in 2010, Jane has had time to focus on work outside of Donatos. Because her roots trace back to the first store on Thurman Avenue on Columbus' south side, she and her family remain committed to the area's success. Evidence of this was the $1.5 million donation that the Grote family contributed to support the city's plan to revive the South Parsons Corridor. She has been an advocate for this project from its inception in 2012 and founded the Reeb Avenue Center, a social-services center housing the Boys and Girls Club, the South Side Learning and Development Center and job-training services.

Jane is a member of the American Heart Association's Go Red for Women and the co-chair for the 2015-2016 Go Red Campaign with husband Tom Krouse. She is a founding member of the Ross Leadership Institute and serves on the Boards of Action for Children, Experience Columbus and I Know I Can. She is also a member of the Columbus Chapter of the Young President's Organization.

Jane has received a number of awards and recognitions. Most recently, she was named to the 2014 YWCA Columbus Academy of Women of Achievement, one of only 237 women so honored since 1986. In 2014, *Columbus CEO* magazine named Jane CEO of the Year and *Franchise Update Magazine* listed her as one of the Top 24 Women in Franchising. Jane was also featured in CBS's hit series *Undercover Boss* where she donned a disguise and went undercover in Donatos restaurants.

Jane and her husband Tom reside in Columbus. She has three children, Tony (age 26), Brianna (age 17) and Tori (age 15); and three stepchildren, Kenny (age 19), Charlie (age 16) and Joey (age 15).